ISLAMIC LAW

SERIES
2

BARR. HAMDALLAH BELLO &
DR JAMIE UMAR CAINE

Paperback: 978-1-965632-23-9
eBook: 978-1-965632-24-6
Library of Congress Control Number: 2024919987

Ordering Information:

Prime Seven Media
518 Landmann St.
Tomah City, WI 54660

Printed in the United States of America

Preface

In the Name of Allah, the Most Compassionate, the Most Merciful.

I slamic law, known as Sharia, is a comprehensive legal system derived from the Quran, the Hadith (the sayings and actions of the Prophet Muhammad, peace be upon him), and centuries of scholarly interpretation. It governs not only religious rituals and practices but also offers guidance on a wide array of societal issues, including family life, business ethics, criminal justice, and governance. As such, it represents a holistic approach to law, embodying principles of justice, equity, and compassion.

This book aims to provide a clear and accessible introduction to the complex and multifaceted nature of Islamic law. It seeks to demystify the foundational concepts and principles that underpin Sharia, while also addressing the diverse interpretations and applications that have emerged throughout Islamic history. By exploring both classical jurisprudence and contemporary issues, this work endeavors to offer a balanced perspective that acknowledges the rich tradition of Islamic legal thought and its relevance in today's world.

The structure of this book is designed to guide the reader through the various dimensions of Islamic law systematically. We begin with an overview of the sources and methodology of Sharia, delving into the Quranic injunctions, the Hadith literature, and the role of Ijtihad (independent reasoning) and Qiyas (analogical reasoning). Subsequent chapters examine specific areas of law, including personal status laws, criminal law, commercial transactions, and international Law. Each chapter includes historical context, key legal principles, and contemporary challenges, providing a comprehensive understanding of how Islamic law operates in different contexts.

One of the key aims of this book is to highlight the diversity within Islamic jurisprudence. The existence of various schools of thought, such as Hanafi, Maliki, Shafi'i, and Hanbali, as well as the contributions of scholars from different cultural and historical backgrounds, illustrates the dynamic and evolving nature of Islamic law. This pluralism is a testament to the intellectual rigor and adaptability of Sharia, which has allowed it to remain relevant across different times and places.

In writing this book, we have drawn upon a wide range of sources and scholarly works, aiming to present a balanced and nuanced account that is both informative and engaging. It is our hope that this book will serve as a valuable resource for students, scholars, and anyone interested in understanding the principles and practice of Islamic law. By fostering a deeper appreciation of Sharia, we aspire to contribute to a more informed and respectful dialogue about its role in the modern world.

We are deeply grateful to the many scholars and mentors who have guided our study of Islamic law, and to our family and friends for their unwavering support and encouragement. May this work be a source of benefit and understanding, and may it inspire further exploration and reflection on the rich tradition of Islamic legal thought.

Peace and blessings be upon the Prophet Muhammad, his family, and his companions.

– Barr. Hamdallah Bello & Dr Jamie Umar Caine
July 2024

Dedication

This book is dedicated to everyone facing oppression all over the world in the 21st century.

Acknowledgements

I am highly indebted to many people for the successful completion of this humble effort, but my unreserved gratitude goes first to Almighty ALLAH (SWT), for His mercy towards the accomplishment of this task which initially seemed unattainable.

My warmest regards go to my mum, dad and siblings, I cherish and love you all.

To my darling husband Dr Jamie Umar Caine for his love, support and understanding, I pray Allah continues to bless our union. To my angels Muttaqin, Muhammad, Ibraheem and Mutaqiyyah indeed, you are all marvellous gifts to me.

To all my mentors: Sheikh (Dr) Ishaq Muhammad Awwal (R.T.A) and all Sheikh Muhammad Al Lawal (RTA)'s family and Khulafah, Amir (Dr) Mohammed Nurudeen Akinwunmi-Othman (Associate Professor-University of the West of England, Bristol, UK), Ustadh Mukadam Sanusi, Sheikh Abd Rasheed Tijani, Sheikh (Dr) Muhammad Ishaq– Oko Awo (Egypt), Sheikh Ishaq Agbarigidoma, Sheikh Omar Niass, and Sheikh Khalil Niass.

To my teachers: Prof. Abdul Kabir Paramole (LASU), Prof. T. Olumoko (LASU), Dr. Lawal Yesufu (Canada), Prof. Moshood Baderin (SOAS), and

Prof. Abdulhakeem Ajonbadi for accepting my proposal to review the book within a very short time frame, I feel a deep sense of gratitude.

To my Awliyah Islamic Academy teachers, the Zawiyah Ahabab Faydotil Awwaliyyah at- Tijaniyyah (ZAFAT-Worldwide) mission board members, Exco and all Mureed and Mureedah, I appreciate you all.

To men of honour and women of goodwill, who have in one way or the other contributed positively to my life, I am grateful to you all.

Barr. Hamdallah Bello

Contents

1. Introduction To Islamic Law

I slamic Law is the comprehensive code of conduct or religious law of Islam governing human being's relationship with their Creator, with his fellow human beings, and with their society and nation. It also deals with the relationship between nations in both war and peace which is the milestone of the modern society's international relations within nations, which are codified into statutes known as International Law.[1]

Islamic Law is derived from two primary sources: the injunctions set forth in the Qur'an, and the example set by Prophet Muhammad (SAW)-peace be upon him (PBUH) in the Sunnah. Fiqh jurisprudence interprets and extends the application of Islamic Law to questions not directly addressed in the primary sources by including secondary sources.

These secondary sources usually include the consensus of the religious scholars embodied in ijma, and analogy from the Qur'an and Sunnah through qiyas. Shia jurists prefer to apply reasoning ('aql) rather than analogy in order to address difficult questions. Regardless of the sect, Muslims believe Islamic Law is God's law.[2]

---

[1]   *The Holy Qur'an (16:36).*

[2]   J. M. Otto. *Sharia and National Law in Muslim Countries: Tensions and Opportunities for Dutch and EU Foreign Policy.* Amsterdam University Press, 2008.

Most jurists divide the study of Islamic Law into two broad categories: 'Devotional Law and Transaction Law'. Basically, these divisions are built upon the fact that the injunctions dealt with by each of these two categories have quite different and distinct primary objectives.

Devotional Law deals with the injunctions that have as their primary objective attaining nearness to Allah, showing Him gratitude, and seeking eternal reward in the Hereafter. This includes prayer, fasting, Hajj, jihad, Zakat, and the fulfilment of covenants. Transaction Law, on the other hand, deals with realizing worldly benefits and regulating human activities, both on the individual and societal level. This covers many branches of law, including Commercial Law and Personal Law. Different views are usually held by the Modernists, traditionalists and fundamentalists in the application of Islamic Law, as they adhere to different schools of Islamic thought and scholarship.

Different countries and cultures have varying interpretations of Islamic Law as well. Islamic Law deals with many topics addressed by secular law, including crime, politics and economics, as well as personal matters such as sexuality, hygiene, diet, prayer, and fasting. Where it enjoys official status, Islamic Law is applied by Islamic judges, or qadis.

The Imam has varying responsibilities depending on the interpretation of the Islamic Law; while the term is commonly used to refer to the leader of communal prayers, the Imam may also be a scholar, religious leader, or political leader. The re-enforcement of Islamic Law is a longstanding goal for Islamist movements in Muslim countries. Some Muslim minorities in Asia (e.g. in India) have maintained institutional recognition of Sharia to adjudicate their personal and community affairs.

In western countries, where Muslim immigration is more recent, Muslim minorities have introduced Islamic family law, for use in their own disputes, with varying degrees of success (e.g. Britain's Muslim Arbitration Tribunal).[3]

---

[3]   *Muslim Arbitration Tribunal.*

1.1 Islamic Law: Definition

Professor Weiss in his publication titled; *The Spirit of Islamic Law*, states that:

> "In archaic Arabic, the term shari'a means 'path to the water hole.' When we consider the importance of a well-trodden path to a source of water for man and beast in the arid desert environment, we can readily appreciate why this term in Muslim usage should have become a metaphor for a whole way of life ordained by God."[4]

Also, Professor Irshad Abdal- Haqq in his own opinion, in *Understanding Islamic Law: From Classical to Contemporary*, states that:

> "Shar'iah, or more properly Al-Shari'ah, literally means the pathway, path to be followed, or clear way to be followed, and has come to mean the path upon which the believer has to tread. In original usage, Shar'iah meant the road to the watering place or path leading to the water, i.e., the way to the source of life. The technical application of the term as a reference to the law of Islam is traced directly to the Qur'an, wherein the adherents of Islam, the believers, are admonished by Allah (God) to follow the clear and right way, the path of Shari'ah: Then we put thee on the (right) Way of religion so follow thou that (Way), and follow not the desires of those who know not."[5]

Also, according to Abdul Mannan Omar in his Dictionary of the Holy Quran, the word Sharia derives from the "Quranic root" shara'a. Derivations include: Shara'a (as prf. 3rd. p.m. sing.), meaning "He ordained", appearing once in the Qur'an at verse 45:13; Shara'u (prf. 3rd. p.m. plu.) "They decreed

---

4   B. Weiss. *The Spirit of Islamic Law*. Spirit of the laws. University of Georgia Press, 1998. ISBN: 9780820319773.

5   H. Ramadan. *Understanding Islamic Law: From Classical to Contemporary*. Contemporary issues in Islam. AltaMira Press, 2006. ISBN: 9780759109919.

(a law)" appearing once at 42:21; Shir'atun (n.) "Spiritual law", used at 5:48; finally, *Shariatun (act. 2nd. pic. f. sing.) "System of divine law, Way of belief and practice" is used at 45:18.*[6]

Therefore, Islamic Law (Sharia) is a crystine path derived from the Qur'an (word of God), Sunnah (examples from the life of Prophet Muhammad (PBUH) and Fatwas (the rulings of Islamic Scholars). Unlike other laws that concentrate largely on matters relating to: Crime, Contract, Civil relationship and individual rights, Islamic Law encompass all aspect of human affairs.

1.2 Branches of Islamic Law

Islamic Law can be broadly divided into five main branches:

1. Ibadah (ritual worship)
2. I'tiqadat (beliefs)
3. Adab (morals and manners),
4. Mu'amalat (transactions and contracts)
5. 'Uqubat (punishments).

In the book "**Reliance of the Traveller**", an English translation on the Shafi'i School of Jurispudence (Fiqh) written by Ahmad ibn Naqib al-Misri, he organizes Islamic law into the below subtopics which has integrated the five branches above:

Purification, Prayer, The Funeral Prayer, The Poor Tax, Fasting, The Pilgrimage, Trade, Inheritance, Marriage, Divorce, Justice.

A times, there are substantial differences in the implementation of the Islamic Law between different schools of Islamic jurisprudence, countries and cultures, in some areas of the aforementioned topics.

---

[6]   A. M. Omar. *Dictionary of the Holy Qur'an.* NOOR Foundation International Inc., 2006.

1.2.1 Purification

In Islam, purification has both spiritual and physical dimension respectively. Muslims believe that certain human activities, contact with impure animals and substances cause impurity. Classic Islamic law details how to recognize impurity and how to remedy it.

Muslims use water for purification in most circumstances, although earth can also be used under certain conditions. Prior the observation of prayer or other religious rituals, Muslims must clean themselves in a prescribed manner.

The manner of cleansing, either 'Wudhu or Ghusl', depends on the circumstance. Muslims' cleaning of dishes, clothing and homes are all done in accordance with stated laws.[7]

1.2.2 Prayer (Salat), Fasting & Pilgrimage

Prayer (Salat)

Muslims are enjoined to pray five times each day. These obligatory prayers (salat) are performed during prescribed periods of the day; and most can be performed either alone or in congregation. There are also voluntary prayers which can be performed, as well as special prayers for certain seasons, days and events.

Muslims must face the Ka'aba in Makkah when they pray, and they must perform purification which is a prerequisite for observing prayers in order for their prayers to be acceptable. Classic Islamic law details many aspects of the act of prayer, including who can pray, when to pray, how to pray, and where to pray.[8]

---

[7] A. I.-N. Al-Misri. *The Reliance of the Traveller (edited and translated by Nuh Ha Mim Keller)*. Amana Publications, 1994.

[8] Ibid.

Fasting

During the Islamic month of Ramadan, Muslims abstain from food, drink, sex, between dawn and sunset. Exceptions to this obligation are made for the young, the aged, and women during their periods of menstruation.[9]

During Ramadan, the daylight hours will often begin and end with a large meal. After dinner, many Muslims participate in special communal prayers held during Ramadan. The end of Ramadan fasting is celebrated with special prayers, gatherings of family and friends, and specially prepared meals. Muslims may also fast on other special days of the year and to make up for missed days of fasting. Classic Islamic law details the exact definition of the fast, the time of fasting, how a fast may be broken, who must fast, and permitted exceptions to the fast.[10]

Pilgrimage

At least once in each Muslim's lifetime, a Muslim if capable in both health and finance must perform holy pilgrimage to Ka'aba, which is the Holy Place of Islam located in Makkah, Saudi Arabia, in fulfilment of last pillar of his religion. The focus of this journey is the Ka'aba, a small rectangular building around which a huge mosque has been built. This pilgrimage, known as the Hajj, begins two months after Ramadan each year. Dressed in symbolically simple clothing, Muslim pilgrims circumcise the Ka'aba seven times, often followed by a drink from a special stream.

Next, a symbolic search for water is performed by travelling back and forth between two nearby peaks. On the eighth day of the Hajj month called Dhul-Hijjah, the pilgrims travel to Mina in the desert and spend the night under tents. The following day, millions of Muslim pilgrims gather on the slopes of Mount Arafat, where the afternoon is spent in prayer.

The Feast of Sacrifice, celebrated by Muslims worldwide, is performed by pilgrims in Mina the following day, and includes the slaughter of animals.

---

[9] Ibid.
[10] C. Horrie and P. Chippindale. *What is Islam?: A Comprehensive Introduction.* Virgin, 2007. ISBN: 9780753511947.

Finally, each pilgrim performs a ritual, tossing pebbles at three symbolic pillars. Classic Islamic law details the manner in which the pilgrim dresses, behaves, arrives, departs and performs each of these rituals.[11]

1.2.3 Funeral prayer (*Janazah*)

Muslims are encouraged to visit those among them who are sick and dying. Dying Muslims are reminded of God's mercy, and the value of prayer, by those who visit them. In turn, the visitors are reminded of their mortality, and the transient nature of life. Upon death, the Muslim will be cleansed and shrouded in clean, white cloth.

A funeral prayer (Janazah) is performed for the deceased, preferably by the assembled Muslim community. The corpse is taken to a designated place which has ground set aside for the burial of Muslims.

The grave is dug perpendicular to the direction of Qiblah and the body is lowered into the grave to rest on its side, with the face turned towards Qiblah. Classic Islamic law details visitation of the ill, preparation of the dead for burial, the funeral prayer and the manner in which the Muslim is buried.[12]

1.2.4 Taxation, Trade and Economics

Taxation

The Quran stipulates that all Muslims, employed or self-employed, must pay taxes to their Government. The Qur'an mentions it in the following verse: *'Know that whatever of a thing you acquire, a fifth of it is for Allah, for the Messenger, for the near relative, and the orphans, the needy, and the wayfarer...'*.[13] The word *'Khums'* is used literally meaning 'one-fifth or

---

[11] Al-Misri, *The Reliance of the Traveller (edited and translated by Nuh Ha Mim Keller)*.
[12] Al-Misri, *The Reliance of the Traveller (edited and translated by Nuh Ha Mim Keller)*.
[13] *The Holy Qur'an (8:41)*.

20%.[14] In Islamic legal terminology, it means 'one-fifth of certain items which a person acquires as wealth, and which must be paid as taxes.'

Income tax for individuals is set at 20% and corporate tax is set at 20% tax on profits.[15] Tax on goods and services such as Value Added Tax and Sales Tax is forbidden in Islam. Property tax, Council Tax, Inheritance Tax and Capital Gains Tax are permitted.[16]

Other Taxes

All Muslims who live above the subsistence level must pay an annual poor tax, known as Zakat. In the modern sense, this would be Islam's equivalent to US Social Security or UK tax system which is usually deducted only after an individual must have earned above a particular threshold per week.[17]

Under Islamic Law, this is not charity, but rather an obligation owed by the Muslim to the poor of the community. The amount is calculated based on the wealth of the Muslim paying the tax, not their income.

The base rate of taxation is 2.5 percent, but it varies depending on the type of wealth being assessed. Wealth includes savings, jewellery and land. Classic Islamic law details the tax, how it is assessed, its collection and distribution.[18]

Trade and Economics

Islamic law recognizes private and community property, as well as overlapping forms of entitlement for charitable purposes, known as awqaf or trusts. Under Sharia law, however, ownership of all properties ultimately

---

[14]   S. M. Rizvi. *Khums, Islamic Tax*. Zakat and Khums (Charity). Accessed July 11, 2024. Al-Islam.Org, 1992. URL: https://www.al-islam.org/printpdf/book/export/html/11184.

[15]   Ibid.

[16]   A. Mahadi, J. E. Saba' Radwan, and L. Burhanuddin. "Shariah View on Consumption Tax: Malaysian GST and SST as Case Studies." In: *Malaysian Journal of Consumer and Family Economics* 22 (2019), pp. 1–14. URL: https://majcafe.com/wp-content/uploads/2022/11/Article-3-Vol-22-2019.pdf.

[17]   Horrie and Chippindale, *What is Islam?: A Comprehensive Introduction*.

[18]   Al-Misri, *The Reliance of the Traveller (edited and translated by Nuh Ha Mim Keller)*.

rests with God; while individual property rights are upheld, there is a corresponding obligation to share, particularly with those in need.[19]

The laws of contract and obligation are also formed around this Qur'anic requirement, prohibiting unequal exchanges or unfair advantage in trade. On this basis, interest on loans is prohibited, as are other transactions in which risks are borne disproportionately to the potential returns between parties to a transaction.

The limits on personal liability afforded by incorporation are seen as a form of usury in this sense, as seen in insurance dealings. All these inequities in risk and reward between parties to a transaction, known collectively as (riba) meaning interest, are prohibited.[20]

For this reason, Islamic banking and financing is a form institutionalised partnership between customers and financial institutions, where risks and gains are distributed equitably.

Partnership, rather than corporations, is the key concept in collective Islamic business. Financing and investments are accomplished in this manner, as purchases and resales, with equity shifting over time between the institution and the client as payments are made or returns are recognized. Conversely, no individual is shielded from the consequences of poor judgement or bad timing.[21] The Islamic financial and investment models have taken root in the West and begun to flourish, even as the financial underpinnings of large Western corporations collapse under the weight of unevenly distributed risks.[22]

---

[19] H. Glenn. *Legal Traditions of the World: Sustainable Diversity in Law*. Oxford University Press, 2014. ISBN: 9780199669837.

[20] Ibid.

[21] Ibid.

[22] J. Crotty. "Structural causes of the global financial crisis: a critical assessment of the 'new financial architecture'". In: *Cambridge Journal of Economics* 33.4 (July 2009), pp. 563–580. ISSN: 0309-166X. DOI: 10.1093/cje/bep023. eprint: https://academic.oup.com/cje/article-pdf/33/4/563/4818627/bep023.pdf. URL: https://doi.org/10.1093/cje/bep023.

Classic Islamic law details the manner of contracting, the types of transactions, the assignment of liability and reward, and the responsibilities of the parties in Islamic trade.[23]

1.2.5 Marriage, Polygamy, Divorce, Child Custody and Inheritance

Marriage

The laws governing Islamic marriage vary substantially between sects, schools, states and cultures. There are two types of marriage: **Nikah** and **Nikah Mut'ah**. The first is more common; it aims to be permanent, but can be terminated by the husband in the talaq [divorce] process or by the wife seeking divorce using khul'.

In **Nikah** the couples inherit from each other. A dowry known as Mahr is given to the bride, a legal contract is signed when entering the marriage, and the husband must pay for the wife's expenses. For the contract to be valid there must be two witnesses under Sunni jurisprudence. There is no witness requirement for Shia contracts. In Sunni jurisprudence, the contract is void if there is a determined divorce date in the Nikah, whereas, in Shia jurisprudence, Nikah contracts with determined divorce dates are transformed into **Nikah Mut'ah**.[24]

While Shia doctrine considers Nikah Mut'ah to be a second form of marriage. The Sunnis scholars contend it as an "Haram". It is a fixed-term marriage which is a marriage with a preset duration, after which the marriage is automatically dissolved. Traditionally the couple does not inherit from each other; the man usually is not responsible for the economic welfare of the woman. Nikah Mut'ah does not count towards the maximum of four wives the Quran allows to Muslim men.[25]

---

[23] Al-Misri, *The Reliance of the Traveller (edited and translated by Nuh Ha Mim Keller)*.
[24] Ibid.
[25] Ibid.

The woman is still given her dowry (Mahr), and the woman must still observe the - iddah, a period of three months at the end of the marriage where she is not permitted to remarry in the case, she may have become pregnant before the divorce took place. Hence, this maintains the proper lineage of children.

Requirements for Islamic Marriages:[26]

- The man who is not currently a fornicator may marry only a woman who is not currently a fornicatress.
- Woman from the people of the Book.
- The woman who is not currently a fornicatress may marry only a man who is not currently a fornicator.
- The fornicator may marry only a fornicatress.
- The Muslim woman may marry only a Muslim man.
- Permission for a virgin female to marry must be given by her guardian, usually her father.
- Any Muslim woman may demand her guardian marry her to a Muslim male, provided he is suitable. If the guardian refuses, a judge will institute the marriage.[27]
- The father, or in some cases the paternal grandfather, may choose a suitable partner for a virgin girl.[28]
- The guardian may not marry the divorced woman or the widow if she did not ask to be married.
- It is obligatory for a man to give bride wealth (gifts) to the woman he marries – "**Do not marry unless you give your wife something that is her right**."

---

[26] S. Fathi. *Gods and Religions*. Writers Republic LLC, 2023. ISBN: 9798891004665. URL: https://books. google.pt/books?id=-B3-EAAAQBAJ.
[27] Al-Misri, *The Reliance of the Traveller (edited and translated by Nuh Ha Mim Keller)*.
[28] Ibid.

Polygamy

In Islamic law, a Muslim man is permitted up to four wives under the Islamic law. All wives are entitled to separate living quarters at the behest of the husband and if possible all of them should receive equal attention, support, treatment and inheritance. In the recent time, it is uncommon for a Muslim man to have more than one wife. Equally, the practice of polygamy has been regulated in some Muslim states.[29]

Historically, Muslim rulers have often remarried the wives of their conquered opponents in order to gain ties of kinship with their new subjects. In these cases, the wives of leaders have sometimes numbered in tens or even hundreds.

In Ottoman Turkey, the practice also filtered down to the aristocracy. This became the basis for the Western image of a powerful, wealthy Muslim.[30]

Divorce

The laws governing divorce vary substantially between sects, schools, states and cultures. The following outline is general in nature.

A marriage can be terminated by the husband in the **talaq** process, or by the wife seeking divorce through **khul'**. Under **faskh** a marriage may be annulled or terminated by the qadi judge. Men have the right of unilateral divorce under classical Islamic Law.

A Sunni Muslim divorce is effective when the man tells his wife that he is divorcing her, however a Shia divorce also requires four witnesses.[31] Upon divorce, the husband must pay the wife any delayed component of the dower.

If a man divorces his wife in this manner three times, he may not re-marry her unless she first marries, and is subsequently divorced from, another man. Only then, and only if the divorce from the second husband

---

[29]   Fathi, *Gods and Religions.*
[30]   Horrie and Chippindale, *What is Islam?: A Comprehensive Introduction.*
[31]   Horrie and Chippindale, *What is Islam?: A Comprehensive Introduction.*

is not intended as a means to re-marry her first husband, may the first husband and the woman re-marry.[32]

In practice, unilateral divorce is only common in a few areas of the Islamic world. It is much more common for divorces to be accomplished by mutual consent. If the wife asks for a divorce and the husband refuses, the wife has a right, under classical Islamic Law, to divorce by khul'.[33] Although this right is not recognized everywhere in Islam, it is becoming more common.[34] In this scenario, the qadi (judge) will effect the divorce for the wife, and she may be required to return part, or all of her dowry.[35]

Under faskh, a qadi judge can end or annul a marriage.[36] Apostasy, on the part of the husband or wife, ends a Muslim marriage in this way. Hardship or suffering on the part of the wife in a marriage may also be remedied in this way. This procedure is also used to annul a marriage in which one of the parties has a serious disability.[37]

Except in the case of a khul' divorce initiated by a woman, the divorced wife generally keeps her dowry from when she was married. A divorced woman is given child support until the age of weaning. The mother is usually granted custody of the child. If the couple has divorced fewer than three times (meaning it is not a final divorce) the wife also receives spousal support for three menstrual cycles after the divorce, until it can be determined whether she is pregnant. Even in a threefold divorce, a pregnant wife will be supported during the waiting period, and the child will be supported afterwards.[38]

---

[32]   *The Holy Qur'an (2:230).*
[33]   Fathi, *Gods and Religions.*
[34]   Horrie and Chippindale, *What is Islam?: A Comprehensive Introduction.*
[35]   *The Holy Qur'an (35:3).*
[36]   Ibid.
[37]   Fathi, *Gods and Religions.*
[38]   Ibid.

Child custody

In a divorce, the child will stay with the mother until the child is weaned, or until the age of discernment, when the child may choose whom it lives with. The age of discernment is 7 or 8 years.[39]

Inheritance

The rules of inheritance under Sharia law are intricate, and a female's share is generally half the amount a male would receive under the same circumstances, This is so because it is considered the responsibility of the males in the family to take care of the women, their sisters (if they are unmarried) and their mothers.[40]

However, up to one third of a person's property may be distributed as bequests, or wasiyya, upon their death. After debts must have been settled, the remainder of the estate will be divided among the family of the deceased according to the rules of inheritance (wasiyya).[41]

In Islamic societies, inherited wealth and property do not easily accumulate to, or remain in, certain families. Large concentrations of property will be divided into smaller portions over time among male inheritors. Property will tend to flow to other families as female inheritors take their shares into their marriages.[42]

Classic Islamic law details the division of property, the shares family members are entitled to, adjustments and redistributions in the shares, orders of precedence among inheritors, and substitution among inheritors.[43]

---

[39]   *The Holy Qur'an (57:25).*
[40]   Horrie and Chippindale, *What is Islam?: A Comprehensive Introduction.*
[41]   Al-Misri, *The Reliance of the Traveller (edited and translated by Nuh Ha Mim Keller).*
[42]   M. Hodgson. *The Classical Age of Islam.* The Venture of Islam: Conscience and History in a World Civilization. University of Chicago Press, 2009. ISBN: 9780226346861.
[43]   Fathi, *Gods and Religions.*

1.2.6 **Justice System**

The concept of justice embodied in Islamic Law is different from that of secular Western law.[44] Muslims believe the Sharia law has been revealed by God. In Islam, the laws that govern human affairs are just one facet of a universal set of laws governing nature itself.

Violations of Islamic law are offenses against God and nature, including one's own human nature. Crime in Islam is sin. Whatever crime is committed, whatever punishment is prescribed for that crime in this world, one must ultimately answer to God on the Day of Judgement.[45]

1.3 **Islamic Law and Jurisprudence**

The formative period of Islamic jurisprudence (Fiqh) stretches back to the time of the early Muslim communities. In this period, jurists were more concerned with pragmatic issues of authority and teaching than with theory. Progress in theory happened with the coming of the early Muslim jurist Muhammad (PBUH) ibin Idris ash-Shafi'i (767-820), who laid down the basic principles of Islamic jurisprudence in his book *Al-Risala*. The book details the four roots of law (Qur'an, Sunnah, *ijma*, and *qiyas*) while specifying that the primary Islamic texts (the Qur'an and the *Hadith*) be understood according to objective rules of interpretation derived from careful study of the Arabic language.[46]

A number of important legal concepts and institutions were developed by Islamic jurists during the classical period of Islam, known as the Islamic Golden Age, dated from the 7th to 13th centuries.[47]

---

[44]   Horrie and Chippindale, *What is Islam?: A Comprehensive Introduction*.
[45]   *The Holy Qur'an (8:41)*.
[46]   Weiss, *The Spirit of Islamic Law*.
[47]   G. M. Badr. "Islamic Law: Its Relation to Other Legal Systems". In: *The American Journal of Comparative Law* 26.2 (Apr. 1978), pp. 187–198. ISSN: 0002-919X. DOI: 10.2307/839667. eprint: https://academic.oup.com/ajcl/article-pdf/26/2/187/10481802/ajcl0187.pdf. URL: https://doi.org/10.2307/839667.

1.3.1 Categories of Human Behaviour

Fiqh classifies behaviour into the following types or grades: fard (obligatory), Mustahabb (recommended), Mubah (neutral), Makruh (discouraged), and Haram (forbidden). Every human action belongs to one of these five categories.[48]

Actions in the Fard (Obligatory) category are those required of all Muslims. They include the five daily prayers, fasting, articles of faith, obligatory charity, and the hajj pilgrimage to Makkah.[49]

The Mustahabb (recommended) category includes proper behaviour in matters such as marriage, funeral rites and family life. As such, it covers many of the same areas as civil law in the West. Sharia courts attempt to reconcile parties to disputes in this area using the recommended behaviour as their guide.[50]

All behaviour which is neither discouraged nor recommended, neither forbidden nor required is of the Mubah (permissible) category. Makruh (discouraged) category, while it is not sinful in itself, the behaviour is considered undesirable among Muslims. It may also make a Muslim liable to criminal penalties under certain circumstances.[51]

Haram (forbidden) category, such behaviour is explicitly forbidden. It is both sinful and criminal. It includes all actions expressly forbidden in the Qur'an. Certain Muslim dietary and clothing restrictions also fall into this category.[52]

The recommended, permissible and discouraged categories are drawn largely from accounts of Prophet Muhammad (PBUH) (SAW). Thus, to say behaviour is Sunnah is to say it is recommended as an example from the life and sayings of Muhammad (PBUH). These categories form the basis for

---

[48]   Horrie and Chippindale, *What is Islam?: A Comprehensive Introduction.*
[49]   Ibid.
[50]   Ibid.
[51]   Ibid.
[52]   Ibid

proper behaviour in matters such as courtesy and manners, interpersonal relations, generosity, personal habits and hygiene.[53]

1.4 The Schools of Islamic Jurisprudence

The schools originated in different places, and it had some impact on their decisions and methods. In the early Islamic periods, the Governors would appoint qadis to judge the subjects of their newly acquired territories.

They had to base their decisions on the Qur'an and act according to what they knew to be the Sunnah (sayings, teachings and practices of Prophet Muhammad (PBUH)), but when none of these sources were available, they had to judge themselves based on their knowledge of Qur'an and Hadith; whatever seemed right to them personally. This usually included considerations of what was customary in the area. Judgment based on own opinion became common practice of the early jurists, and a system of logic to support the decisions was being formed.

The Classical Schools of Sunni Islamic

The four schools (Madhaib) of Sunni Islam are each named by students of the classical jurist who taught them. The Sunni schools (and where they are commonly found) are:

- Hanafi (Turkey, Pakistan, Central Asia, Indian subcontinent, Afghanistan, China and Egypt)
- Maliki (North Africa, the Muslim areas of West Africa, and several Arab states of the Persian Gulf)
- Shafi'i (Arabia, Indonesia, Malaysia, Maldives, Egypt, Somalia, Eritrea, Ethiopia, Yemen and southern parts of India)
- Hanbali (Saudi Arabia).

---

[53]   Ibid

These four schools share most of their rulings, but differ on the particular Hadith they accept as authentic and the weight they give to analogy or reason (qiyas) in deciding difficulties.

1.4.1 The Hanafi School

The Hanafi School: It was the earliest founded under the jurist Imam Abu Hanifa (700-768), whose real name was Nu'man ibn Thabit. He was born in the city of Kufa (modern day Iraq). The Hanafi school based its rulings largely on the results of logical deductions by scholars.

1.4.2 The Maliki School

It was founded under Imam Malik (713-797). His real name was Abu Abdullah Malik bin Anas; He was born in Madinah which reflects in his decisions. The Maliki School ruled heavily in favour of the practice of the local community of Madinah, where the immediate descendants of Prophet Muhammad (PBUH)'s followers lived.

1.4.3 The Shafi'i School

It was founded under Imam Ash-Shafi'i ((767-820) He was the first to systematise Islamic law. He originally studied both in Iraq and in Madinah, but disagreed with the methodology of the older schools He seemed to be in favour of the Traditionalists but did not fully accept their ideas either.

In his tractate, the "Risala", balancing the two trends, he laid down the sources of Law, Usul al-Fiqh and his system had become the basis of Islamic jurisprudence that was subsequently used by all the schools. He instituted the four components in order of priority as follows:

1. The Qur'an
2. The Sunnah of the Prophet Muhammad (PBUH)

3. Ijma (consensus of the Muslim community)
4. Qiyas, (reasoning by analogy), including Istihsan

1.4.4 The Hanbali School

It was founded under Imam Ahmad Ibin Hanbal (781-856)A.D., who had followed Shafi'i school method with ever greater emphasis on the Hadith, avoiding reasoning as far as possible, but not completely denying it.

2. Development of Islamic Law

F undamentally, during the 19th century, the history of Islamic law took a sharp turn due to new challenges the Muslim world faced: the West had risen to a global power and colonized a large part of the world, including Muslim territories. In the Western world, societies changed from the agricultural to the industrial stage, new social and political ideas emerged, and social models slowly shifted from hierarchical towards egalitarian. The Ottoman Empire and the rest of the Muslim world were in decline, and calls for reform became louder. In Muslim countries, codified state law started replacing the role of scholarly legal opinion.

2.1 Historical Account and Stages in the Development of Islamic Law

Western countries do inspire but sometimes pressurize and force Muslim states to change their laws. Secularist movements pushed for laws deviating from the opinions of the Islamic legal scholars. Islamic legal scholarship remained the sole authority for guidance in matters of rituals, worship, and spirituality, while they lost authority to the state in other areas. The Muslim community became divided into groups reacting differently to the change.

Secularists believe that the law of the state should be based on secular principles, not on Islamic legal doctrines.

Traditionalists believe that the law of the state should be based on the traditional legal schools. However, traditional legal views are considered unacceptable by some modern Muslims, especially in areas like women's rights or slavery.

Reformers believe that new Islamic legal theories can produce modernized Islamic law and lead to acceptable opinions in areas such as women's rights. However, traditionalists believe that any departure from the legal teachings of the Qur'an as explained by the Prophet Muhammad (PBUH) and put into practice by him is an alien concept that cannot properly be attributed to "Islam".

Stages in the Development of Islamic Law

The Prophet (SAW) did not leave this world until after the edifice of the Islamic Law was completed and its basis and general principles fully outlined. This has been established by a clear text from the Quran:[1]

> Today, I have perfected for you your religion and completed my favour upon you and have chosen for you Islam as your religion.
>
> - Qur'an 3:5

At the same time, the Prophet (SAW) did not leave a fully codified Law for his Companions. He left them with only a collection of principles and general rules and a number of specific injunctions and judicial verdicts that are found in the Quran and Sunnah. This would almost have been sufficient for them if the authority of Islam had not spread beyond the confines of the Arabian Peninsula and met with circumstances and customs that the Muslims had never encountered before.

---

[1]   *The Holy Qur'an (3:5).*

When this happened, they disagreed on how these new factors fit in with the general principles of Islamic Law, its injunctions, and its objectives. That which is contained in the Qur'an was a set of principles, the understanding of which was capable of being broadened and advanced with the broadening of the scope of human thought and the appearance of the new circumstances that Islam had to deal with when it came in contact with other cultures and customs. At this point in time, the Muslim scholars began to investigate issues and, in a religious light, derive laws for the circumstances of a more informed life.

This advancement in the organization of Islamic Law was the result of the work of the Caliphs and those that followed them in accordance with what was suitable for the circumstances.

In the newly opened territories where foreign peoples began entering the fold of Islam in droves, there was a pressing need to instruct them in the things that they were ignorant of and to clearly define the injunctions of the Sharia. It was also necessary to apply these injunctions in a way that would properly regulate human interaction and clearly define the peoples' rights.

In this way, Islamic Law advanced over the ages, each successive generation contributing to its growth, until it became a great and awesome edifice, regulating in detail every type of human interaction and relationship.

One who follows the historical development of Islamic Law will observe that it passed through different stages with respect to its formation, growth, and development over the past fourteen centuries.

The writings in Law for every school of thought have seen development since the era of their founders, passing through different styles, from commentaries on original texts, to summaries and abridged works, and then to the great legal encyclopaedias.

Thereafter, writings began in the field of defining general axioms of Islamic Law that included comparing and grouping injunctions according to patterns evident in the legislations. The field of Comparative Law also developed, as well as Legal Theory, the codification of definitions, and the formulation of formal legal codes.

Development of Islamic Law:

1. The prophetic era, comprising the life of the Prophet Muhammad (PBUH) (SAW). This era saw the completion of the edifice of the Islamic Law and the perfection of the Islamic religion.

2. The era of the four rightly guided Caliphs and the period that followed it up to the middle of the first century A.H. This period and the one that preceded it are considered the preliminary stage for the codification of Islamic Law.

3. The era from the middle of the first century A.H. to the beginning of the second century. At this stage, Islamic Law became a distinct science of its own that scholars specialised in. Schools of thought were formed in this period, which is the stage that Islamic Law as a science was established.

4. The fourth era starts from the beginning of the second century to the middle of the fourth. During this stage, the codification of Islamic Law was completed.

5. The fifth era is from the middle of the fifth century to the fall of Baghdad at the hands of the Tatars in the middle of the seventh century. At this stage, the writings in the field of Islamic Law started to become rigid.

6. The fifth era from the middle of the seventh century to the beginning of the modern era. This stage is one of weakness with regard to the methodologies employed in the codification of Islamic Law.

7. The era from the middle of the thirteenth century A.H. to the present day. During this period, studies in Islamic Law broadened considerably, especially in the field of Comparative Law and in the critical study of the major classical works in the field.

2.2 Objectives of Islamic Law

"*Objectives of Islamic Law*", is referring to the general aims that Islamic Law strives to fulfil with respect to human life as well as the specific aims targeting legal injunctions have been set down in order to achieve. Therefore, these objectives can be classified into two broad categories: general and specific.

The *general objectives of Islamic Law* are those that aim at realizing the general human welfare, both in this world and in the Hereafter, this is achieved by the legislation of a body of legal injunctions.

The *specific objectives of Islamic Law* are those that Islamic Law seeks to realize in a narrower domain of human activity, such as economics, family life, or the political order. Which is achieved through specific legislation aimed at dealing with particular issue in that regard.

All the revealed religions and all rational people agree that the most important way to ensure human welfare is through the preservation of five universal necessities. These are: faith, life, reason, lineage, and wealth.

Islamic Law provides all the injunctions needed to protect and preserve all these five necessities. Islamic Law legislates what is needed to ensure their existence in human society as well as what is needed to develop them and preserve them from being corrupted and/or lost.

The Preservation of Faith

Islam has stressed the importance of faith for human life by inciting the natural human inclination to worship Allah, man's religious sentiments and inner feelings, the strength of the elements of goodness and virtue as well as the prosperity and tranquillity that faith affords man.[2] Due to these factors, faith is a vital necessity of human life.

---

[2]   *Religion*. Tech. rep. Accessed July 11, 2024. 2016. URL: https://techraifa.blogspot. com/2016/12/ chapter-1-religion-concept-of-religion.html.

Qur'an says:[3]

> So set your face towards the pure faith, Allah's natural way upon which He created mankind. There can be no change in Allah's Creation. This is the straight faith, but most men do not know.
>
> - Qur'an 30:30

Bridgestone stated thus:

> "There have been – and continue to be – human societies that do not possess science, art, or philosophy, but there has never been a society without religion.[4]"

In consideration of these factors, Islamic Law protects faith. In some cases, this is achieved by planting faith firmly and deeply in the heart and mind. In other cases, this is through nurturing the seed of faith that is already present in an individual and supporting it with what will develop it and make it endure. As a means to achieving these goals, Islam has established the following:

1. **Faith are established on a clearly defined articles:** The articles of faith are as follows: belief in Allah, His Messengers, His Books, His angels, the Day of Judgment, and belief in destiny and pre destiny, (both good and bad).

   Qur'an says:[5]

> The Messenger believes in what was sent down to him from his Lord, and so do the believers. All of them believe in Allah, His angels, His books, and His Messengers. (They say:) We make no distinction between any of the Messengers.
>
> - Qur'an 2:285

---

[3]   *The Holy Qur'an (30:30).*
[4]   *Religion.*
[5]   *The Holy Qur'an (2:285).*

Qur'an also says:[6]

> O you, who believe, believe in Allah, His Messenger, the Book that was sent down upon the Messenger, and what was sent down before. Whoever disbelieves in Allah, His angels, His books, His Messengers, and the Day of Judgment has gone far astray.
>
> - Qur'an 4:136

2. **Faith is established on the basis of knowledge and rational proofs:** On these grounds, Islam calls towards examination, contemplation and reflection.

    Qur'an says:

> Do they not look into the dominion of the heavens and the Earth and all the things that Allah has created? Allah reproaches those who do not reflect upon the many signs that are present in Creation, saying: How many a sign in the heavens and Earth they pass by while they are aversely turned away.

He also reproaches those who follow their desires and blindly follow their forefathers in belief without having any proof at hand and without engaging in any contemplation.

Qur'an says:[7]

> When it is said to them, 'Follow what Allah has sent down' they say, 'Nay! We shall follow what we found our fathers following.' Would they do this even though their fathers did not understand anything nor were they guided?
>
> - Qur'an 5:104

---

6   *The Holy Qur'an (4:136).*
7   *The Holy Qur'an (5:104).*

3. **The pillars of Islam must be established:** These pillars are the principal acts of worship that Islam enjoins upon the believers. The first of these is to make an open testimony of one's Islam. This is then followed by prayer, Zakat, fasting, and performing the Holy pilgrimage.

   Among the most important effects of these acts of worship – and the profound wisdom behind them – is that they create a direct bond between the worshipper and his Lord, strengthening and rejuvenating the faith that exists in the heart of the believer.

   Allah's Messenger (peace be upon him) relates that Allah says:[8]

   > The servant does not seek nearness to Me with anything more beloved to Me than what I have commanded him to do. Then the servant continues to seek nearness to Me with voluntary acts until I love him.
   >
   > - Hadith Nawawi 38

   Allah's Messenger (peace be upon him) relates that Allah says:[9]

   > The servant does not seek nearness to Me with anything more beloved to Me than what I have commanded him to do. Then the servant continues to seek nearness to Me with voluntary acts until I love him.
   >
   > - Hadith Nawawi 3

4. **It is a duty to call others to Islam:** This duty extends to maintaining and sponsoring such efforts, and to giving due support and protection to those who are carrying it out.

---

[8] *Nawawi 38 related by Al-Bukhari on the authority of Abu Hurayrah.* Hadith 38.

[9] *Nawawi 3 related by Al-Bukhari and Muslim on authority of Abdullah, the son of Umar Al-Khattab.* Hadith 3.

Qur'an says:[10]

> Let their arise from amongst you a group of people who invite to all that is good, command what is right and prohibit what is wrong . These are the successful ones.
>
> - Qur'an 3:104

Qur'an also says:[11]

> Invite to the way of your Lord with wisdom and good exhortation and argue with them in the best manner.
>
> - Qur'an 16:125

Qur'an mentions the advice that Luqman gave to his son:[12]

> O my son, perform the prayer, command what is right, and prohibit what is wrong, and bear patiently whatever befalls you.
>
> - Qur'an 31:17

5. **The Means taken to maintain and Preserve Faith:** What is meant here are the methods pursued by Islamic Law to protect and safeguard faith after it has been achieved, to maintain its purity in the heart, and to remove any obstacles from its path. Among these means are the following:

---

[10]   *The Holy Qur'an (3:104).*
[11]   *The Holy Qur'an (16:125).*
[12]   *The Holy Qur'an (31:17).*

Islam guarantees and protects freedom of religion

Islam does not compel anyone to embrace it and permits a plurality of religious beliefs to coexist under its authority within the boundaries of the Islamic state. It affords the people of other faiths the freedom to maintain their beliefs, religious practices, and civil codes.

Allah's Messenger (peace be upon him) relates that Allah says:

> They have the rights that we have and the duties that we have.

Furthermore, one of the goals of jihad (struggle in the cause of Allah) is to protect religious freedom.

Qur'an says:[13]

> Had it not been for Allah checking one people by means of another, monasteries, churches, synagogues, and mosques, wherein Allah's name is often mentioned, would have been torn down.
>
> - Qur'an 22:40

Islam prescribes Jihad to defend the faith, repel its enemies, and to protect it.

What is meant here is another method pursued by Islamic Law to protect and safeguard faith from distortion.

Qur'an says:[14]

> Fight in the path of Allah against those who fight you and do not transgress bounds; verily Allah does not love the transgressors.
>
> - Qur'an 2:190

---

[13] *The Holy Qur'an (22:40).*
[14] *The Holy Qur'an (2:190).*

Qur'an also says:[15]

> What is wrong with you that you do not fight in the path of Allah and for the weak and oppressed men, women, and children whose cry is, 'Our Lord, rescue us from this town whose people are oppressors, and raise for us from Your grace one who will protect us, and raise for us from Your grace one who will help us.
>
> - Qur'an 4:75

1. **After accepting Islam, it is obligatory to adhere to the teachings of the faith and to put them into practice:**

    This gives faith vitality in the hearts of its practitioners and makes it have its effect on their sentiments. Because of this, belief and good works are mentioned together in many verses of the Quran, wherein the following phrase is repeated quite frequently:[16]

> What is wrong with you that you do not fight in the path of Allah and for the weak and oppressed men, women, and children whose cry is, 'Our Lord, rescue us from this town whose people are oppressors, and raise for us from Your grace one who will protect us, and raise for us from Your grace one who will help us.
>
> - Qur'an 103:3

Apostasy is a crime punishable by law. This ensures that a person is serious when embracing Islam, so that no one enters into the fold of Islam without first having firm and complete conviction. Moreover, Allah does not accept anyone's faith unless it springs from conviction.

---

[15]   *The Holy Qur'an (4:75).*
[16]   *The Holy Qur'an (103:3).*

If a person enters Islam, it must be a permanent decision taken on the basis of firm conviction. If he rejects faith thereafter, he is actually introducing to the public a measure of intellectual and political uncertainty that can disrupt society and destroy its desired level of intellectual and psychological stability.

Qur'an mentions the words of the idolaters who called to these activities:[17]

> A group of the People of the Scripture said: "Believe in what came down upon those who believe at the beginning of the day, then disbelieve at the end of the day, so perhaps they might return from faith".
>
> - Qur'an 3:72

Thus, the punishment for apostasy was legislated to safeguard the seriousness and the sacredness of faith.

2. **A number of necessary and complementary acts of worship have been established to act as a protective shield for one's faith:**
   Among these are performing prayers in congregation and numerous forms of voluntary worship. These acts establish and ingrain faith within the hearts of the people who perform them and strengthen faith in the society where these acts are put into practice. This brings to both the individual and the society a sense of security, tranquillity, and righteousness.

The Preservation of Life

The sanctity of human life is one of the necessities of human existence. Islam has set down a number of means to secure the sanctity of life. Among these are the following:

---

[17]   *The Holy Qur'an (3:72).*

The means taken to promote the existence of human life: Islamic Law prescribes marriage. Islam legislated it for the purpose of producing progeny, increasing the human population, and providing people who will develop the Earth and sow the seeds of human life for the generations to come. Islam extols the sacred relationship between a husband and wife and considers it to be one of Allah's signs.

Qur'an says:[18]

> Among His signs is that He created for you wives from among yourselves that you may find comfort in them, and He has put between you affection and mercy.
>
> - Qur'an 30:21

The means taken to safeguard the continuity of life:

- **Islam obligates man to secure the means to sustain his life**. This includes obtaining food, drink, clothing, and shelter. It is forbidden for a Muslim to eschew these necessities to the point where it endangers his life. It also obligates the state to provide the minimum amount of these necessities to those who are incapable of providing for them. Furthermore, it obligates one who is in danger of losing his life to prevent death by consuming the property of others to the extent of his need.

- **The state is obligated to furnish the necessary infrastructure to ensure public safety. This includes such things as providing a justice system and a police force.**

- **It is obligatory to defend the honour of the human being.** This manifests itself in such laws as the prohibition of false accusation and defamation. It is also why restricting human activities without

---

[18]   *The Holy Qur'an (30:21).*

justification is prohibited. In this way, liberties such as freedom of thought, freedom of opinion, economic freedom, the freedom to reside where one wants to, and the freedom to relocate are safeguarded and ensured.

Qur'an says:[19]

> Whoever abuses believing men and women undeservedly, they bear upon themselves the crime of slander and manifest sin.
>
> - Qur'an 33:58

- **Islamic Law provides concessions under certain conditions to ward off undue difficulty that might cause personal harm or injury.** One of these concessions is the right of the one who is sick or travelling to break his fast during Ramadan. Another is the right of the traveller to shorten his prayers.

- **Islam prohibits the taking of human life, whether that life is one's own or that of someone else.**

  Qur'an says:[20]

> Do not kill yourselves. Verily Allah is to you Most Merciful.
>
> - Qur'an 4:29

The crime of murder is deplorable, so much so that taking one life is considered equivalent to killing all of mankind.

---

[19]   *The Holy Qur'an (33:58).*
[20]   *The Holy Qur'an (4:29).*

Qur'an says:[21]

> Whoever kills a person, not in retaliation for murder or iniquity in the Earth, and then it would be as if he killed all of mankind.
>
> - Qur'an 5:32

Qur'an also says:[22]

> Do not kill a person whose life Allah has made sacred except in the dispensation of justice.
>
> - Qur'an 6:151

Qur'an says:[23]

> Whoever kills a believer intentionally, his recompense is Hell, abiding therein. Allah's wrath is upon him, and His curse; and He has prepared for him a great punishment.
>
> - Qur'an 4:93

In an authentic Hadith, it is related that Allah's Messenger (peace be upon him) said:[24]

> Whoever kills someone who has a covenant with us will never smell the fragrance of Paradise.
>
> - Hadith (Al-Bukhari and Muslim)

---

[21]   *The Holy Qur'an (5:32).*
[22]   *The Holy Qur'an (6:151).*
[23]   *The Holy Qur'an (4:93).*
[24]   *Al-Bukhari and Muslim (www.eaalim.com>Home>Blog). Hadith.*

Retribution is prescribed in the case of murder while payment of blood money and freeing a slave are obligatory in the case of unintentional manslaughter:

Qur'an says:[25]

O you who believe, the law of retribution is prescribed for you in murder.

- Qur'an 2:178

Qur'an says:[26]

It is not for a believer to kill another believer except by mistake; and whosoever kills a believer by mistake must set free a believing slave and pay blood money to the deceased family unless they remit it. If the deceased belonged to a people at war with you and he was a believer, then a believing slave must be set free; and if he belonged to a people with whom you have a treaty, then blood money must be paid to his family and a slave must be freed. And whoever finds this (the freeing of a slave) beyond his means must fast for two consecutive months seeking repentance from Allah. And Allah is All-Knowing, All-Wise.

- Qur'an 4:92

- **Jihad may be proclaimed in order to preserve lives and safeguard those who are weak and oppressed on Earth.**

  Qur'an says:[27]

What is wrong with you that you do not fight in the path of Allah and for the weak and oppressed men, women, and children.

- Qur'an 4:75

---

[25] *The Holy Qur'an (2:178).*
[26] *The Holy Qur'an (4:92).*
[27] *The Holy Qur'an (4:75).*

- **Islamic Law prescribes self-defence when one is attacked.**

  One should defend oneself if attacked and the defender is not in any way responsible if the attacker dies, as long as it is clear that the other truly intended to attack him.

The Preservation of Reason

Islam affords a great deal of importance to reasoning since it is the basis on which human beings are held responsible for their actions. Reason is the attribute that honours the human being and exalts him above the rest of Creation. It is what qualifies him to be Allah's vicegerent on Earth and to carry out the sacred trust from Allah.

Qur'an says:[28]

> Verily, We had offered the trust to the heavens and the Earth and the mountains, but they declined to bear it and were afraid of it. But man bore it.
>
> - Qur'an 33:72

Due to its extreme importance, Islamic Law seeks to preserve reason and establishes a number of injunctions to ensure the health and freedom of the rational faculties. Among these are the following:

- Islam has prohibited every substance that affects the mind, harms it, or decreases its abilities: This includes substances like wine and hashish. Qur'an says:[29]

> O you who believe, intoxicants, gambling, sacrificing to idols and divination are an abomination of Satan's handiwork. So avoid all of this that perhaps you might be successful.
>
> - Qur'an 5:90

---

[28]   *The Holy Qur'an (33:72).*
[29]   *The Holy Qur'an (5:90).*

- Islam sets down a stiff legal punishment to discourage the use of intoxicants: This is on account of the serious danger that they pose to both the individual and society.

- Islam develops the intellect and nurtures it on a spirit of independent thinking: It guides the intellect to understand, to contemplate, to follow rational arguments and proofs, and to discard the attitude of following others blindly.

  Qur'an says:[30]

Or have they taken for worship gods beside Him? Say (O Muhammad (PBUH)): "Bring your proof.

- Qur'an 21:24

Qur'an also says:[31]

Whoever invokes besides Allah another god, of whom he has no proof, and then his reckoning is only with his Lord. Verily, the disbelievers will not be successful.

- Qur'an 27:64

The Qur'an declares to the unbelievers:[32]

Bring your proof, if you are truthful.

- Qur'an 27:64

---

[30] *The Holy Qur'an (21:24).*
[31] *The Holy Qur'an (27:64).*
[32] Ibid.

- **Islam calls toward developing and cultivating the mind.**

   On the material level, this includes getting proper nourishment that strengthens the body and enlivens the mind. For this reason, it is disliked for a judge to pass judgment when he is hungry. This is also the reason why, if food happens to be served at the time of prayer, it is preferable to eat before going to perform the prayer. On the intellectual level, Islam emphatically encourages the pursuit of knowledge, considering it to be the basis of faith.

   Qur'an says:[33]

> It is only the knowledgeable among His servants who fear Allah.
>
> - Qur'an 3:190

Allah commands us to offer the following supplication:[34]

> Say, 'O my Lord, increase me in knowledge.
>
> - Qur'an 39:9

Qur'an says:[35]

> Verily those who dispute about Allah's signs without any authority having come to them, they have nothing in their hearts except pride. They shall never attain it. So seek refuge in Allah, Verily, He is the All-Hearing, All-Seeing.
>
> - Qur'an 40:56

---

[33]   *The Holy Qur'an (3:190).*
[34]   *The Holy Qur'an (39:9).*
[35]   *The Holy Qur'an (40:56).*

- Use of reason should be based upon a fruitful manner of gathering information and drawing conclusions; and upon a firm grasp of the facts.

There are two approaches to this:

Rational investigation: Islam has set down the proper method for rational investigation, one that provides certainty. This means that Islam calls to confirming things, facts and/or issues before believing them.

Qur'an says:[36]

> And follow not that which you have no knowledge.
>
> - Qur'an 17:36

Qur'an also makes reference to the youths who sought refuge from their people by going to the cave:[37]

> These people of ours have taken for worship gods beside Allah. Why, then, do they not bring a clear proof for them? So who does more wrong than he who invents a lie against Allah?
>
> - Qur'an 18:15

Reflection and contemplation: Islam calls to reflection and contemplation about the laws of nature, encouraging humanity to bring them to light and appreciate their intricacy and how deeply they are interrelated. It also calls to induction based on careful observation and detailed examination in order to attain certainty.

---

[36] *The Holy Qur'an (17:36).*
[37] *The Holy Qur'an (18:15).*

- Islam directs the mind to seek out the wisdom and subtleties behind its legislations: Qur'an says:[38]

> Do they not, then, carefully consider the Qur'an? Had it been from other than Allah, they would surely have found within it many contradictions.
>
> - Qur'an 4:82

- Likewise, Islam directs the intellect towards attaining knowledge of the physical world and how to benefit from it in order to build civilization.
  Qur'an says:[39]

> He is the one who has made the Earth subservient to you; so walk in its land and eat of His provision.
>
> - Qur'an 47:24

- **Islam has left open the door of juristic reasoning with respect to its legislation wherever there is a matter for which there is no direct textual evidence.**
  There are two areas where this can occur, which are stated below:

  — Ascertaining the aims and objectives of the texts and legal injunctions.
  — Deriving legal injunctions for newly occurring problems and situations: This is a very broad area that takes recourse to a number of general principles, like juristic analogy, considering the general welfare, and juristic preference as earlier discussed.

---

[38]   *The Holy Qur'an (4:82).*
[39]   *The Holy Qur'an (47:24).*

The Preservation of Lineage

Lineage, here, is understood to mean the continuation of the human race through the agency of hereditary descent. Islam strives to perpetuate the human life on Earth until the Last Day. In order to bring about this objective, Islam has set down the following principles and legislations:

- **Islam enjoins marriage:** Fundamentally, Islam permits and encourages marriage, considering it to be the pure and natural way for a man and a woman to come together. It is for the purpose of preserving the human species and producing righteous offspring who will develop the world, establish an exemplary model of human life, and assume the role of Allah's vicegerent on Earth.

- **Islam pays close attention to child upbringing:** In order to ensure proper upbringing, parents are obliged to take care of their children and provide for their needs until they no longer need their parents' support.

- **Islam establishes the family on a firm foundation, considering it to be the stronghold that protects and enhance the next generation:** Islam establishes the marital bond on the basis of harmonious dealings between the two spouses and mutual consultation on all matters. This brings feelings of affection and mutual understanding between them, causing each of the two spouses to seek the happiness of the other.
  Allah says:[40]

Among His signs is that he created for you wives from among yourselves that you may find comfort in them, and He has put between you affection and mercy.

- Qur'an 30:21

---

[40]   *The Holy Qur'an (30:21).*

● **Islam safeguards all possible relationships between men and women with a collection of principles and codes of moral conduct:** Islam ensures that the noble aims of the relationships are protected and destructive practices in relationships between the sexes are avoided. Among these obligations is the duty of every man to avert his gaze from every woman and for every woman to avert her gaze from every man. This helps to prevent sexual desire from being ignited. Likewise, Islamic Law combats the causes of temptation by making concealing clothing of a specific quality obligatory on the Muslims. Outside of terrible necessity, Islam prohibits a man to be alone with a woman to whom he is not related by blood, fosterage, or marriage, even if proper dress is observed, unless she is accompanied by one of her close relatives.

The home necessarily enjoys a great deal of sanctity in Islam, whereby it is forbidden to enter another's home without seeking the permission of its occupants and greeting them with peace. Qur'an says:[41]

> O you who believe, do not enter houses other than your own before seeking their permission and greeting their occupants with peace.
>
> - Qur'an 24:27

Added to these and other etiquettes, Islam provides codes of conduct when interaction between unrelated men and women becomes necessary.

● **Islam forbids assault on chastity and honour:** Islam forbids fornication and adultery, as well as falsely accusing someone of sexual iniquity, setting fixed, prescribed punishments

---

[41]   *The Holy Qur'an (24:27).*

for both of these crimes in order to discourage them. With regard to fornication.

Qur'an says:[42]

> The woman and man guilty of illegal sexual intercourse flog each of them with a hundred stripes. Do not let pity dissuade you from carrying out a punishment prescribed by Allah.
>
> - Qur'an 24:2

Qur'an says:[43]

> And those who accuse chaste women and fail to produce four witnesses, flog them with eighty stripes, and reject their testimony forever.
>
> - Qur'an 24:4

The Preservation of Wealth

Islam permits individual ownership, while at the same time providing the necessary legislation to prevent the harmful effects that this inclination would have if left unchecked, like the loss of social equilibrium and the concentration of wealth within a small sector of society.

Some of the systems that Islam has put in place to fulfil this function are those of Zakat, inheritance, and social security. From this perspective, Islam considers wealth to be a one of the indispensable necessities of human life.

Islam has set down for man laws and guidelines that encourage him to seek a livelihood and acquire wealth, and secure for him its safety, preservation, and growth. This is achieved through the following steps:

---

[42]   *The Holy Qur'an (24:2).*
[43]   *The Holy Qur'an (24:4).*

- The means taken to ensure the production and acquisition of wealth:

  - **Islam encourages actively seeking ones sustenance and earning a livelihood:** Islam considers the earning of wealth, if pursued with a righteous intent and with permissible means to be a form of worship and a means of achieving closeness to Allah.

    Qur'an says:[44]

    > He is the one who has made the Earth subservient to you; so walk in its land and eat of His provision.
    >
    > - Qur'an 47:24

    Qur'an also says:[45]

    > Then when the prayer is completed, set forth in the Earth and seek the bounty of Allah.
    >
    > - Qur'an 62:10

  - **Islam raises the status of work and elevates the standing of the workers:** In an authentic Hadith, Allah's Messenger (SAW) said:[46]

    > No one has ever eaten food better than that which he has earned with the work of his own hands. The Prophet of Allah, David, used to eat from the work of his own hands.
    >
    > - Hadith (Al-Bukhari and Muslim)

---

44   *The Holy Qur'an (47:24).*
45   *The Holy Qur'an (62:10).*
46   *Al-Bukhari and Muslim (www.eaalim.com>Home>Blog).*

Islam establishes the right to work for every individual and holds the state responsible to provide work for those who are unable to find it. Islam, also, asserts the honour and nobility of the worker and makes his material and intangible rights to be an obligation. Allah's Messenger (peace be upon him) said:[47]

> Give the worker his wage before his sweat has time to dry.
>
> - Hadith (Al-Bukhari No: 2109)

He also said:[48]

> There are three who I will speak against on the Day of Judgment: a man who was entrusted with something then betrayed the trust, a man who sold a free person into slavery and took the price, and a man who hired a worker and benefited from him then did not pay his due.
>
> - Hadith (Bulugh al Maram 1285)

- **Islam permits just forms of commercial transactions:** It allows transactions that are neither oppressive to any of the parties concerned nor infringe upon the rights of others. For this reason, we find that that Islam reaffirmed many types of transactions that were already in existence before Islam, after ridding them of any element of oppression.

  These include numerous transactions such as selling, loaning on collateral, and partnerships. Islam also opens the door for new forms of transactions that the accumulated experiences of society might uncover; provided that they contain no element of oppression or injury to any of the parties involved and that they do not entail wrongfully consuming the wealth of others.

---

[47]   *Al-Bukhari*. Hadith 2109.
[48]   *Bulugh al Maram*. Hadith 1285.

- **The Means Taken to Ensure the Preservation and Continuation of Wealth:**

  - **The use of wealth is limited by the constraints of considering the general welfare:** Therefore, any means of acquiring wealth that is unlawful and harmful to others is expressly forbidden. One such means is the collection of interest, because of the detrimental effect that it has on social equilibrium. Qur'an says:[49]

> Allah has permitted commerce and forbidden interest.
>
> - Qur'an 2:275

  Qur'an also says:[50]

> Do not consume each other's wealth unjustly.
>
> - Qur'an 2:188

  - **Islam prohibits transgressing against the wealth of others through theft, burglary, or fraud:** Islam sets a fixed punishment for theft. Hence, the aim of this is to serve as a deterrent. Qur'an says:[51]

> The thieves, male and female, cut off their hands.
>
> - Qur'an 4:27

---

[49]   *The Holy Qur'an (2:275).*
[50]   *The Holy Qur'an (2:188).*
[51]   *The Holy Qur'an (4:27).*

Thus, it is obligatory on anyone who damages the property of others to pay compensation.

Allah's Messenger (peace be upon him) said:[52]

> The blood, wealth and honour of every Muslim are sacred.
>
> - Hadith (Al-Arba 'ina Hadithan An-Nawawiyyah No:14)

- **Islam forbids wealth to be spent in unlawful ways and encourages spending in the way of charity:** This is based upon one of the most important principles of the Islamic economic system: All wealth belongs to Allah alone, and man is merely entrusted with its use.

Qur'an says:[53]

> And spend from that which He has made you trustees.
>
> - Qur'an 63:10

Qur'an also says:[54]

> Also, and give them from Allah's wealth that He has bestowed upon you.
>
> - Qur'an 65:7

Hence, it is incumbent upon anyone who possesses wealth to use his wealth within the confines set by Islamic Law. It is not permissible for him to let his wealth tempt him into

---

[52] *Al-Arba 'ina Hadithan An-Nawawiyyah.* Hadith 14.
[53] *The Holy Qur'an (63:10).*
[54] *The Holy Qur'an (65:7).*

transgression, because this is a cause of degradation and destruction.

Qur'an says:[55]

> When We decide to destroy a town, We send a command to those among them who live a life of luxury. Then, they commit sin therein, and thus the word is justified against them and We completely annihilate it.
>
> - Qur'an 17:16

It is likewise impermissible for him to squander his wealth on useless things. Qur'an says:[56]

> Do not squander, verily those who squander are the brethren of the devils.
>
> - Qur'an 17: 26-27

- **Islamic Law provides legislation to protect the wealth of the mentally deficient and others who are incapable of managing their own wealth:** This includes the wealth of orphans and minors until they reach the age of discretion. For this reason, a guardian is appointed to manage their wealth. Qur'an says:[57]

> Test the orphans until they reach the age of marriage and if you find them of sound judgment, then release their property over to them.
>
> - Qur'an 4:6

---

[55]   *The Holy Qur'an (17:16).*
[56]   *The Holy Qur'an (17: 26-27).*
[57]   *The Holy Qur'an (4:6).*

Qur'an also says:[58]

> They ask you concerning the orphans. Say (O Muhammad (PBUH)): "The best thing is to improve their property.
>
> - Qur'an 2:220

This principle also encompasses placing an interdiction over the property of a mature person who, nevertheless, is incapable of exercising proper judgment with regard to the disposal of his property.

Qur'an says:[59]

> Do not give to the foolish your property that Allah has given you to maintain, but feed and clothe them from it and speak to them words of kindness.
>
> - Qur'an 4:5

- **Financial interactions are structured around the principles of consent and justice:** Islam, thus, maintains that contracts are not binding unless the contracting parties exercise their mutual consent and the contract's provisions are just. For this reason, gambling is prohibited.

Qur'an says:[60]

> O you, who believe, do not consume each other's property unjustly, but let there be commerce between you by mutual consent.
>
> - Qur'an 4:29

---

[58]   *The Holy Qur'an (2:220).*
[59]   *The Holy Qur'an (4:5).*
[60]   *The Holy Qur'an (4:29).*

● **Islam encourages wealth to be invested and developed so that it can fulfil its proper function in society:** Fundamentally, Islam prohibits and combats the hoarding of wealth and keeping it out of circulation.

Qur'an says:[61]

> And those who hoard up gold and silver and do not spend them in the way of Allah announce to them a painful punishment.
>
> - Qur'an 9:34

With all these injunctions, Islam protects wealth and safeguards it from corruption so it can fulfil its necessary and indispensable role in the order of human life and facilitate the growth of civilization. Its place is just like that of the other necessities of life, for together they form the basis of human life and civilization. If they are not properly managed and preserved, the world economy could collapse.

2.3 Distinctive Characteristics of Islamic Law

Anyone who follows Islamic Law or studies will discover that it is distinguished by certain characteristics and unique qualities that are not shared by any other legal entity. These characteristics have allowed its enjoyment in terms of stability, growth, and relevance over centuries.

The reason for this is that Islamic Law has a permanent and global character because the religion of Islam is believed to be the last in the line of divinely revealed religions. It is, thus, necessary for Islamic Law to have certain unique qualities that afford the continuity and stability it needs to

---

[61] *The Holy Qur'an (9:34).*

deal with the ever-changing requirements of human life over vast stretches of time and space.

Islamic Law, with its distinctive features, is unprecedented in the history of Law. It was applied, through various schools of thought, from one end of the Muslim World to the other. It also had a great impact on other nations and cultures. Many nations of the world borrowed their own legal systems from Islamic Law by way of contact with Islamic Spain, Sicily, Turkestan, Bukhara, and the Balkans. In today's time, it is considered one of the sources of world law.

Some of the unique characteristics of Islamic Law are the following:

2.3.1 Nobility of Purpose of the Islamic Law

Every system of law has an objective behind it that it seeks to fulfil. The principles that it follows are established with the sole aim of realizing this objective. This objective varies from culture to culture. It also varies due to the changing aims and objectives of those in power with legislative authority. For this reason, changes and amendments are commonplace, due to the fact that nations employ law as a means of directing their citizenry to certain objectives.

Likewise, the state employs law as a means of achieving certain limited goals where the political authority has no other means at its disposal to bring them to realization. Islamic Law, on the other hand, is not shaped by society; rather, society is shaped by it. This is because man did not create it, but in fact, recreates himself in conformity to society.

Islamic Law is not limited to regulating the interrelationships between individuals in society. First and foremost, it regulates the relationship between the individual and the Creator by legislating different forms of worship like prayer, fasting, Zakat, and Hajj. Moreover, it defines the rights and obligations each individual has with respect to others, so that the potential harm any individual might cause to others is effectively negated. In this regard, Allah's Messenger (peace be upon him) said:[62]

> There should be no harm and no harming of others.
>
> - Hadith (Al-Arba 'ina Hadithan An-Nawawiyyah No:24)

In fact, Islamic Law aims at the greatest objective which is that of realizing the benefits and best interests of both the individual and society and warding off what would be detrimental, giving preference neither to the needs of the individual nor to those of society as a whole.

2.3.2 Islamic Law as a divine revelation

All the injunctions of Islamic Law are revelations from Allah, so the one who is legislating for mankind is their Creator who knows best what will be of benefit to his creation in both this world and the next. He knows the psychological makeup of the human being, what will be in harmony with it, and what will clash with it.

Qur'an says:[62]

> Does the One who created not know, and he is the Gentle, the All-Aware.
>
> - Qur'an 67:14

As limited power is subject to deficiency and error. This is the reason that the intellect can never truly comprehend the human soul and what is in harmony with the nature that Allah has placed within it. Therefore, the legislations that come from human effort may not always be suitable for human nature.

---

[62]   *Al-Arba 'ina Hadithan An-Nawawiyyah*. Hadith 24.
[62]   *The Holy Qur'an (67:14)*.

Applying the injunctions of Islamic Law constitutes obedience to Allah

Following the injunctions of Islamic Law is belief to be a way of worshipping Allah and earning His reward. Likewise, disobeying the Law is a belief that amounts to disobedience of Allah and is a way of deserving of His wrath. Some forms of transgression have prescribed punishments that are supposed to be carried out in this world. Others hold the threat of punishment in the Hereafter.

It is, thus, possible for us to say that the individual Muslim is always acting as an overseer policing himself out of fear of Allah. It is on this basis the character of the individual and society is built.

As for man-made laws, the impetus to obey them is the fear of reprisal from the political authority, not the hope of attaining blessings and rewards from Allah. Likewise, disobedience to such laws does not instil a feeling of wrongdoing as long as it goes unnoticed by the authorities. Thus, there is nothing to discourage the use of deception to assert a legal claim against someone else, because whatever the judge rules will be deemed permissible or forbidden, in the most absolute sense, on the basis of his judgment.

Islamic Law is distinct by being comprehensive and general in its scope

Islamic Law regulates three different factors: the relationship between an individual and his Lord, the relationship between an individual and himself, and the relationship between an individual and others. Devotional Law deals with the first of these through its legislation of different forms of worship, like prayer and fasting securing the relationship between the individual and his Lord.

Thus, the relationship between the individual and himself is handled by injunctions like those dealing with dietary laws, those regulating personal dress, and everything else that is legislated for the purpose of protecting the individual, his mind, and his body.

While the relationship between the individual and others is regulated by transaction Law and the prescription of punishments to be carried out in this world by the state. It covers such things as marriage, buying and selling, leasing, retribution, fixed punishments, discretionary punishments, legal verdicts, and testimony.

The regulation of all three of these concerns assures that Islamic Law deals with every aspect of human life. In Islamic Law, this is expressed in terms of the five necessities: **"life, religion, reason, honour, and property"**. All Islamic legislation does refer back to the preservation of one or more of these five necessities.

The notion of "separation of church and state" is not premised in Islamic Law as one of its fundamental components. Ethics is another fundamental principle. The comprehensiveness of Islamic Law manifests itself in its direct concern for every stage in an individual's life.

From the time that he is in the womb until the time that he is born, then throughout his infancy, adolescence, adulthood, and old age, and even up to his death and beyond, Islamic Law protects and safeguards the rights of human beings all through. It assures these rights, even when the individual is unable to assert them by himself, like while he is in the womb, or is in his infancy, or after death.

Islamic Law, also, protects the rights of the rationale adult without any discrimination as well as its concerned with the future of the human being, not only in this world but also in the hereafter, by enjoining acts of worship that must be carried out by every believer in the Islamic faith.

Stability in Principles and Flexibility in the Application of Islamic Law

Islamic Law is planted upon, unchanging principles derived from the Quran and Sunnah. The texts of the Qur'an and Sunnah have been most carefully and accurately recorded and preserved. Most of these texts contain general injunctions for legislation without going into the precise details relating to its application. This affords the jurists broad powers of discretion that allow them to take ever-changing circumstances into consideration.

The Islamic political system is a good example. The religious texts give a general outline of how it should be, which includes such things as justice between the citizenry, obedience to political authority, consultation between Muslims, and co-operation in righteous conduct.

At the same time, the texts leave the application of this general outline to practical circumstances that require a measure of flexibility. The most important thing is that the outlined objectives of the Islamic government are realized, not the manner in which they are carried out or the different forms that this might take, so long as the injunctions imposed by the sacred texts and the principles of the Islamic Law are not violated.

In carrying out the objectives of Islamic Law, there is a great degree of flexibility and a tremendous capacity for development. There is nothing to prevent the appearance of new injunctions that were previously unknown, in response to changing requirements. The jurists refer to this as the principle that legal injunctions change with the changing of time and place. With this principle, Islam leaves the door to juristic discretion open, allowing the jurist to refer all the matters that the texts are silent about back to similar issues where the texts have given a ruling.

Added to this is the fact that, in Islamic Law, customary practice and the consideration of the general welfare are two important secondary sources of legislation. These two sources are themselves, quite capable of keeping the injunctions harmonious with the cultural environment in which they occur.

The permanence and stability of these basic principles and the flexibility allowed in their application give Islamic Law a distinct attribute not shared by any other modern legal system, due to this fact, most of the other legal systems, as they attempt to respond to the needs of the day through continuous revision and reform, the foundations and principles of most of these legal systems are exposed to change and substitution so much that they become the targets of corruption for some of those who are in the position to set down such legislation.

The absence of Difficulty and the Limitation of Imposition in Islamic Law

Islamic Law does not impose any obligations of great severity or difficulty. Nothing in Islamic Law is overly burdensome. Whoever scrutinizes the injunctions of Islamic Law will find within them a clear tendency towards alleviating difficulties. He or she will also find that all obligations that have been imposed, from the onset, have had leniency and ease taken into consideration for the ones who must carry them out.

Allah has commanded that every legally accountable person must perform prayer five times a day, with no individual prayer requiring more than a few minutes. The one who is unable to stand is permitted to sit.

There is an equal degree of leniency in fasting. Fasting is obligatory for one month out of the year. The difficulty in carrying it out does not reach the level of any real hardship. In spite of this, breaking the fast is permitted for the one who is travelling or is ill. Consumption of meat that has not been properly slaughtered is forbidden but may be eaten in cases of dire necessity.

Expiations have been provided to compensate for certain sins. There are many other things that point to the fact that Islamic Law aims at achieving ease and removing difficulties in its legislation so that people will not find themselves incapable of doing their obligations which have been enjoined upon them for their own benefit.

Qur'an says:[63]

> O you who believe, do not ask about things that if they were made clear to you would cause you harm. If you ask about them when the Quran is being revealed, they will be made clear to you. Allah has forgiven them, and Allah is Forgiving, Forbearing. Those before you asked about them then became disbelievers.
>
> - Qur'an 5:101

---

[63]   *The Holy Qur'an (5:101).*

Allah had forbidden the people from delving into issues and becoming severe with them so that this would not cause certain injunctions to become obligatory that otherwise would not have been made compulsory. This would have led to a greater number of obligations that the people would be incapable of carrying out. This would have caused them to fall into ruin. This verse alludes to the fact that Allah intended to make the number of obligations small in order to make carrying them out easy for us and so that we would not fall into undue hardship.

The Richness and all-encompassing effect of Islamic Law

Anyone who studies Islamic Law will find that it contains an abundance of material and a wealth of ideas. This is evident in the various opinions of the jurists and the number of schools of thought. In spite of their large number, their differences, and their diversity, none of them go outside the general scope of Islamic Law.

Moreover, there are numerous schools of thought from the earliest generations of Islamic scholars. All of this instituted that Islamic Law is not limited to the opinions of one scholar or those of a specific group of people. Quite the contrary, it is a collection of opinions that ultimately all stem from the Quran and Sunnah.

This richness is one of the factors that give Islamic Law the ability to develop, grow, and respond to the growth of human civilization. It prevents Islamic Law from becoming rigid and stagnant. This diversity, in reality, stems from disagreement in understanding the same body of textual evidence, thus, it is a form of disagreement that offers diversity, non-antagonism, and contradiction.

The richness of Islamic Law also manifests itself, in the encyclopedic books where its injunctions are recorded in great precision and detail, treating even the rarest cases and sometimes even posing hypothetical situations that have not yet occurred, in order that the injunctions will be readily available.

Additionally, the jurists have explored the general tendencies in Islamic Law by studying the injunctions and then deriving general axioms from their patterns, hence, these patterns could be used as guidelines for legal decisions which have become a field of study on its own. However, the numerous injunctions that were studied were themselves derived on the basis of other rules outlined in the separate discipline of Islamic Jurisprudence, which deals with the methods by which legal injunctions can be derived from their original sources.

2.4 The Sources of Islamic Law

What is meant by "the sources of Islamic Law" are the types of evidence that the Lawgiver set down as valid proofs for the injunctions. The jurists unanimously agree upon some of these types of evidence, these being the Quran, the Sunnah, and juristic consensus. The majority of scholars also recognize juristic analogy as the fourth source of evidence.

Hence, added to this are secondary forms of evidence like juristic discretion, customary practice, and the consideration of general welfare. Before discussing these sources of Law in depth, it is appropriate to make it clear that the sources in reality have their origins in one source, which is the Qur'an.

Thus, every source of Law coming after the Qur'an is derived from it. For this reason, al-Shafiʿi, the founder of one of the four orthodox schools of thought, used to say: *The injunctions must be derived only from the sacred texts or related back to them.*

Al-Shafiʿi did not recognize anything except the sacred texts or refer issues back to them. Furthermore, he recognized juristic analogy as the only valid way of referring new issues back to the texts.[64] While, other leading jurists had a broader view of what could be considered a means of referring issues back to the texts, adding all the other possible secondary sources of Law.

---

[64] Imam Muhammad ibn Idris al-Shafi'I. *Al-Shafiis Risala: Treatise on the Foundations of Islamic Jurisprudence*. The Islamic Text Society, 2010.

We shall first discuss the primary sources of Islamic Law – the Quran, Sunnah, juristic consensus, and juristic analogy. Thereafter, we shall deal with the secondary sources – juristic discretion, the consideration of general welfare, and customary practice.

2.4.1 The Qur'an and the Hadith/Sunnah

The Qur'an

This is the origin of all Islamic legislation. It sets forth the fundamentals of the Islamic Law. It clarifies beliefs in great detail and discusses forms of worship and legal matters in broad terms. It fulfils the role in Islamic Law that a constitution fulfils for the man-made laws of nations. This is why the Quran is considered the source of all legislation, even though its role as a "constitution" for Islamic Law limits it to clarifying injunctions in only general terms, rarely dealing with particular details.

The general orders for such things as prayer and the Zakat tax are given in the Quran, without the manner of performance being dealt with. This is then expounded by the words and practices of the Prophet (SAW) as recorded in the Sunnah. Likewise, the Quran, in general terms, orders that contractual obligations be carried out, asserts the permissibility of trade, and prohibits interest. It does not stipulate which types of contracts are valid and which types are invalid. This has been taken up by the Sunnah.

Sometimes the Quran deals with the particulars of its injunctions. It does so with regard to inheritance, the divorce procedure due to an accusation of adultery, certain prescribed punishments, and the prohibited degrees of marriage, among other injunctions that do not change with the passage of time.

The generality of Qur'anic texts provides another important distinction with respect to Civil Law, as well as to the political and social order. It allows for the texts to be understood and applied in various ways, all of which are accommodated by the wording of the texts, making the injunctions capable of responding to the requirements of the general welfare over the course of time without departing from the fundamentals and objectives of the Islamic Law.

Due to their generality, the texts of the Quran need the Prophetic Sunnah to clarify them, so their injunctions can be carried out in the manner and to the limit intended under various circumstances. For this reason, the Qur'an alludes to the Sunnah when it comes to these details, by saying:[65]

> Whatever the Messenger gives you, then take it, and whatever he forbids you, then leave it alone.
>
> - Qur'an 59:7

Based on this passage, the Sunnah becomes a fundamental key to understanding the Qur'anic texts. All Muslims agree that the Qur'an is a source of legislation and that its injunctions must be followed. They also agree that it is the first source to be referred to and that nothing else should be referred to except if the needed injunction is not interpreted therein. It is also accepted that the meaning of its words are in some case unambiguous in its meaning, having only one possible interpretation, and that in other cases multiple interpretations are possible.

The Hadith/Sunnah

This term is used to refer to the statements, actions, and tacit approvals of the Prophet Muhammad (PBUH) (SAW). With this meaning, it is synonymous with the word "Hadith". We might also use the word Sunnah to mean the practical application of the injunctions during the prophetic era.

The Sunnah comes after the Qur'an in its ranking as a source of Islamic Law, as it comes to clarify what the Quran leaves ambiguous or difficult to understand, qualify what the Quran leaves unqualified, and bring up

---

[65]   *The Holy Qur'an (59:7).*

issues that the Qur'an does not mention. An example of the latter is the grandmother's share of inheritance, for it is established that the Prophet (SAW) ruled that the grandmother receives one sixth of the estate.

The Sunnah shows itself to be subsidiary of the Qur'an in another way, for the Sunnah, in addition to its role of providing explanation and clarification, it never departs from the Quran's general principles even when it sets forth injunctions that the Quran does not mention, the Sunnah, in turn, is necessary and indispensable for the proper understanding and application of the Qur'an.

Since the era of prophetic tradition came to an end with the death of the Prophet (peace be upon him), the Sunnah has been transmitted to Muslims by way of narrators. Only the narrations whose authenticity can be established according to the most stringent conditions are acceptable as proof for legislation in Islamic Law. The scholars of the Sunnah expended great efforts in the classification of the prophetic Hadith into Sahîh (authentic), Hasan (good), Da'îf (weak), and Mawdû' (fabricated). Only the first two are acceptable as proof in Islamic Law.

The most prominent and reliable works in the Sunnah are Sahîh al-Bukhari, Sahîh Muslim, Sunah Abî Dawûd, Sunah al-Nas'î, Sunah al-Tirmidhî, and Sunah Ibin Majah. Likewise, the Muwatta' of Imam Malik and the Musnad of Ahmad b. Hanbal hold a position of importance with the scholars of Hadith and Islamic Law.

However, there is no disagreement about the Sunnah being one of the sources for Islamic legislation. It holds a position secondary to that of the Quran in that the Quran takes precedence in providing proof for legislation. When a jurist looks for a ruling on a certain matter, he looks to the Quran first, if he finds the desired injunction therein, he applies it. If not, he takes recourse to the Sunnah, this order of precedence is indicated by the following discussion that the Prophet (peace be upon him) had with Mua'dh: The Prophet (peace be upon him) asked:

"How will you judge if the position is given to you?" Mua'dh said: "I will judge according to the Book of Allah." He then asked: "And if you do not find it in the Book of Allah?" Mua'dh responded: "Then I will judge according to the Sunnah of Allah's Messenger (PBUH)."

Also, it was related that the Caliph 'Umar wrote to the judge Shurayh: "You should judge according to the Book of Allah, and if you do not find what you need in the Book of Allah, then judge according to the Sunnah of Allah's Messenger." It is not known that anyone took exception to this.

2.4.2 Juristic Consensus (Ijma) and Analogy (Qiyas)

Juristic Consensus (Ijma)

This refers to the unanimous agreement of the jurists of a given era on a legal ruling. It makes no difference whether the jurists are from the era of the Companions after the death of the Messenger (peace be upon him) or any era thereafter.

Consensus is a very strong source of evidence for establishing the injunctions of Islamic Law. It comes after the Sunnah in rank. The proof for its validity is drawn from a number of verses and Hadith that show the unanimous statement of the people of knowledge is in itself a valid proof. The verdicts arrived at by consensus are usually drawn from the Quran and Sunnah, it is inconceivable that the reliable scholars of Islam would ever come to agreement on an issue on the basis of personal inclination without there being a proof from the sacred texts establishing it i.e Fatwa.

For this reasons, scholars of later generations, when investigating the possibility of consensus, look for the presence of the consensus and the reliability of how it has been reported without concerning themselves with the textual evidence behind it. If it were necessary to look for the textual proof for every case where consensus took place, then juristic consensus would effectively cease to be a valid proof in that effect.

Juristic Analogy (Qiyas)

This refers to taking an injunction that applies in one case and applying it in another because they share a characteristic, which is the effective cause of the injunction being applied in the first case. Juristic analogy ranks as the fourth source of Islamic legislation, though its effects are more widespread and far-reaching than that of juristic consensus due to the fact that so many injunctions in Islamic Law are based upon it. The reason for this is that the issues where consensus have taken place are few, since there is no way that it could occur after the earliest eras of Islamic history. Another reason for this is that the scholars have become scattered all over the world and have not been able to engage in mutual consultation.

This is not the case for juristic analogy, because it does not require unanimous agreement. Quite the contrary, each jurist uses analogy according to his own, personal reasoning for every new situation that has not been previously addressed by the Quran, Sunnah, or consensus. It should not go unnoticed that the Quran and Sunnah are necessarily limited in the number of issues that they can directly address.

At the same time, the number of new occurrences and expected future occurrences knows no limit. There is no way for Islamic legal injunctions to be established for every new development and every possible transaction except by way of applying the methods of reason, at the forefront of which is that of analogy. Analogy is the most widely applied and versatile sources for extrapolating specific injunctions to deal with new issues confronted by Islamic Law.

The sacred texts generally state the effective cause and the rationale for most of the injunctions that they establish. This facilitates the application of these injunctions in new but similar cases that make their appearance in every age. The texts of the Quran are mostly of a general and universal nature, as we have seen.

This has opened the doors to analogous reasoning, allowing cases that the texts have not treated to be referred back to those that the texts have dealt with decisively by applying the textually established injunctions wherever their effective causes are evident.

The cases handled by way of analogy in Islamic Law are too numerous to count. The greater portion of Islamic legislation is made up of these cases. Analogy continues to be used for every new issue that is not directly addressed by the sacred texts. For example, the texts that deal with injunctions pertaining to an agreement of sale are more than those that deal with a lease agreement. Consequently, the jurists, by way of analogy, took many of the injunctions referring to sales and applied them to lease agreements due to the fact leasing is essentially the sale of rights and benefits.

Likewise, the texts deal at length with the injunctions pertaining to the guardians of orphaned minors, detailing their rights, responsibilities, and capabilities. The jurists, by way of analogy, applied the same injunctions to the executors of endowments, due to the similarities in their duties. They also derived many of the injunctions pertaining to endowments themselves from those that the texts had established for bequests.

2.5 The Supplementary Sources of Islamic Law

There are other acceptable means of deriving Islamic legal injunctions, besides the four primary sources. The Quran and Sunnah have given indications that these sources are also to be considered as credible means of establishing legislation, except that they play a subsidiary and subordinate role to that of the four primary sources.

For this reason the majority of scholars do not count them as distinct sources of law, but merely as extensions of the primary ones. We shall deal with the two most important of these secondary sources: consideration of general welfare and customary practice.

2.5.1 Al-Istihsan

As a juristic term, Istihsan is defined as shifting from one Qiyas to another Qiyas due to a reason or suspending a Qiyas for a reason. In relation to its literal meaning, it is the art of adopting a judgment that is equitable as a diversion from the use of analogy, to a ruling that is in consonance with the broader rules of justice, interest and public good.

A Mujtahid may take into consideration any of these options

- Istihsan by Qiyas - switching from a ruling of Qiyas to another ruling of Qiyas due to a stronger reason.

- Istihsan by necessity - shifting to another Qiyas due to necessity.

- Istihsan by Sunnah - Cancelling the Qiyas due to a contradiction caused by the Hadith.

- Istihsan by Ijma as Sahabah - cancelling a ruling from Qiyas due to a contradiction caused by the Ijma as Sahabah

2.5.2 Consideration of General Welfare (Istislah)

This is establishing injunctions on the basis of public good (Maslaha al Mursalah in Arabic) neither expressly considered nor rejected by the sacred texts. Literally, Maslaha means benefit or interest. As a juristic term Maslaha Mursalah refers to *accepting public interest* in the absence of ruling regarding an issue from the Quran or Sunnah.

Types of Maslaha Al Mursalah

- Maslaha cancelled by the text - Maslaha (interest) which is cancelled due to a ruling from the text.

- Maslaha approved by the Shar'iah - Benefit which the Shar'iah doesn't forbid.

- Adopting Maslaha (benefit) in an action for which there is no ruling from Quran and Sunnah.

There is no debate amongst the Ulama on the first two types of Maslaha al Mursalah. But there is disagreement regarding the third type of

Maslaha. Some have accepted it within specific requirements while others have rejected it outrightly.

The factors that could encourage a jurist to consider the general welfare are as follows:

- **Attaining that which is beneficial:** This means attaining that which society needs so that human life can be maintained in the best, most dignified manner.

- **Avoiding that which is harmful:** This entails avoiding those things that can cause detriment either to the individual or to society, regardless of whether this harm is of a material nature or a moral one.

- **Preventing wrongdoing:** This entails preventing the means by which the commands of the Sharia are neglected or its prohibitions are violated, even if only unintentional.

- **Changing times:** This refers to the changing circumstances people find themselves in. Each of these four factors requires the jurist to resort to considering the general welfare in order to produce new injunctions that can effectively carry out the general objective of the Sharia to establish society in the best manner possible. A good example of the application of this principle is an act initiated by the second Caliph, 'Umar b. al-Khattaab. He established the general registry for the armed forces to set their salaries and their terms of service. He then established registries for other purposes.

  In the same vein are the traffic laws of today that came in response to the demands of the automobile and were set down in order to preserve life and prevent collisions and accidents.

2.5.3 Customary Practice (Istishabul Hal)

The Arabic word 'urf also known as Istishabul Hal' refers to that which is well known, widely accepted, and regarded as correct among those of sound minds. We find it used in the Qur'an in the following verse:[66]

> Show forgiveness, enjoin what is good (al-'urf), and turn away from the ignorant ones.
>
> - Qur'an 7:199

However, it should be clear that something should not be considered customary practice if it is not consistently applicable to all or most of the members of a given population. This means that the majority of the people must take it into consideration and act on its basis.

Thus, it is imperative for the custom to be the general assumption shared by the majority of the people. If it is not the practice of at least the vast majority of the population, then it will only be counted as an act of individual discretion.

Basically, this source is belief to dwell heavily on customs and local usages prevailing anywhere when such is not opposed to the Quranic injunction and not expressly forbidden by the Sunnah. Thus, this source is recognised as close to Ijma as it has its precedence in Qiyas, the Hanafi and the Shafi'i School of thought results to this source on the condition that it is not repugnant to a clear text of the Qur'an or reliable Sunnah.[67]

Thus, the efforts of the Islamic jurists are in agreement regarding the recognition of customary practice, even though they differ greatly in the extent to which they use it. The jurists – especially those of the Hanafi school of thought – have given customary practice considerable weight

---

[66]   *The Holy Qur'an (7:199)*.

[67]   M. Haroon. *An Integrated Introductory Note on Shari'ah Law*. Tech. rep. 14. Lagos, 2001.

in establishing and limiting the rights of people in the domain of legal transactions and other aspects of social behaviour.

However, the Hanafi School of thought considers customary practice, as an important principle and a great source of legislation for establishing rights and obligations wherever it does not contradict the Holy Scripture. To them, customary practice is a valid proof for establishing binding legislation wherever any other proof is not available.

It can as well take precedence over juristic analogy, because applying an injunction based on analogy in conflict with custom might cause undue hardship. In this case, the Hanafi concept of juristic discretion comes into play, which allows for the circumvention of analogous reasoning in some instances.

Hence, if on the other hand, customary practice violates a text of the Qur'an and/ or Sunnah, then the custom is rejected. This includes practices such as consuming usury and the custom of imbibing alcoholic beverages on certain occasions. Practices such as these are rejected outrightly because they are clearly prohibited by the Islamic law.

2.6 Ijtihad

Ijtihad is derived from the root word Jahada. Linguistically, it means striving or self exertion in any activity which entails a measure of hardship. As a juristic term, Ijtihad means exhausting all of one's efforts in studying a problem thoroughly and seeking a solution to it from the sources of the Islamic Law.

A person who performs Ijtihad is known as Mujtahid (pl. mujtahideen) while a person who knows the rules of the Islamic Law in detail, but is unable to extract rules directly from their sources, is not a Mujtahid but rather a Faqih, Mufti, or a Qaadi.

The texts of Qur'anic and Sunnatic texts which are conclusive in meaning provide only one understanding. Any Ijtihad on these types of text will render only one meaning. The texts related to issues such as Riba or murder is clear in their prohibition of these things. No Mujtahid can claim that Riba or murder is allowed because the text only offers one meaning. Finally, he must have a comprehensive knowledge of the issue on which Ijtihad is being performed.

To extract any ruling one has to understand the subject thoroughly. If the Mujtahid doesn't understand an issue, he is not allowed to do Ijtihad regardless of where he lives. To understand the issue, the Mujtahid can go to experts. For instance, there might be an issue in genetic engineering. To understand the process of genetic engineering, the Mujtahid can go to an expert in this field.

Therefore, these criteria are enough to qualify one to do Ijtihad, and it is incorrect to say that each issue requires the Mujtahid to reside in that environment. The Mujtahid can reside anywhere and do Ijtihad as long as he is familiar with the issue being dealt with. If the Mujtahid is not familiar with the issue, he is not allowed to do Ijtihad, even if the issue occurs in the same environment he resides.

2.6.1 Why the difference of opinions among the Mujtahideen?

The word Madhab means "school of thought - Fiqh". The following are some of the reasons for the existence of Madhahib (schools of Fiqh):

Differences in the Legislative Sources

Criteria in evaluating the Sunnah One Mujtahid may consider a certain Hadith authentic while others may not. This is due to their differences in the criteria for judging the authenticity of the Hadith.

- **Differences in the Sahabah's opinions as individuals:** Some scholars accepted the opinion of one Sahabi as a legislative source, while others treated the Sahabah as Mujtahid whose individual opinions were not legally binding except collective opinions.

- **Differences in the practice of Qiyas:** Some scholars practiced Qiyas while others practiced Istihan.

- **Differences in Ijma (Consensus of Opinion):** Some scholars used Ijma as-Sahabah, while others used Ijma Ahlul-Madinah (People of Madinah), Ijma Al-Mujtahideen, and various other types of Ijma.

- **Differences in other legislative sources:** Some Scholars used Maslaha Mursalah while others did not. This contributed to more differences among the scholars.

Differences in interpreting the text itself

- **Literalists:** Some scholars took the literal understanding of the text, meaning that they took the text at its surface value, refusing to take deeper understandings. Some of these scholars were called Zahiris, or those who took only the apparent meanings of the texts.

- Those who saw hidden meanings in the text In addition to the apparent meaning, some Scholars took deeper and implicit meanings in the texts, known as - Batini.

Differences in Methodology of Usul-Fiqh

There were differences in interpreting the forms and types of commands. For example, in the Hadith regarding the beard, there is a difference of opinion among the Scholars regarding whether the Hadith indicates Fard, Mustahab, or Mubah commands.

Differences in Understanding the Arabic Language

This may be due to a different understanding of the Arabic text where it offers more than one meaning.

2.7 Modern Perspectives of the Islamic Law

Muslims have responded in a variety of ways to the forces of modernity which cross across the lines of tradition, sect and school. They affect the way Islamic Law is interpreted by individuals in their personal lives, and the extent to which Islamic Law is implemented in the public sphere by the state. These diverse movements can be referred to collectively as contemporary Sharia(s).[68]

2.8 Spectrum of Islamic legal systems

The legal systems in 21st century Muslim majority states can be classified as follows:

- **Islamic Law in the secular Muslim states:** Muslim countries such as Mali, Kazakhstan and Turkey have declared themselves to be secular States. Here, religious interference in state affairs, law and politics is prohibited.[69] In these Muslim countries, as well as the secular West, the role of Islamic Law is limited to personal and family matters.

- The Nigerian legal system is based on English Common Law and the constitution guarantees freedom of religion with the separation of church and State. However, eleven northern states have adopted Islamic law for those who practice the Islamic religion.[70]

- **Muslim states with blended sources of law:** Muslim countries including Pakistan, Indonesia, Afghanistan, Egypt, Sudan, Morocco and Malaysia have legal systems strongly influenced by Islamic Law, but also accord ultimate authority to their constitutions and the rule of law.

- These countries conduct democratic elections, while politicians and jurists make law, rather than religious scholars. Most of these

---

[68]   J. M. Otto. *Sharia and National Law in Muslim Countries: Tensions and Opportunities for Dutch and Eu Foreign Policy.* Amsterdam University Press, 2008.

[69]   Otto, *Sharia and National Law in Muslim Countries: Tensions and Opportunities for Dutch and Eu Foreign Policy.*

[70]   C. D. Ebeniro. "The Problems of Administration of Justice on Female Offenders in Nigeria". In: *African Journal of Criminology and Justice Studies* 4 (2011), p. 28.

countries have modernized their laws and now have legal systems with significant differences when compared to classical Islamic Law.[71]

- **Muslim states using classical Islamic Law:** Saudi Arabia and some of the Gulf States do not have a separate constitutions or legislatures. Their rulers have limited authority to change laws, since they are based on the Islamic Law as it is interpreted by their religious scholars. Iran shares some of these characteristics, but also has a parliament that legislates in a manner consistent with the Islamic Law.[72]

2.9 Factors influencing the modern role of Islamic Law

Against the backdrop of differing religious sects, scholarship, classical schools of thought, and governmental implementations, the following forces are responsible for influencing future developments in Islamic law.

- **Rapid exchange of cultures and ideas:** Around the world, Muslims are becoming more connected by the Internet and modern communications. This is leading to wider exchanges of ideas and cultures. Reactionary and fundamentalist movements are unlikely to halt this trend, as Islamic Law itself defends the right to privacy within the home.[73]
- **Schools of thought:** Legal scholar L. Ali Khan claims that "the concept of Sharia has been thoroughly confused in legal and common literature. For some Muslims, Sharia consists of the Qur'an and Sunnah. For others, it also includes classical Fiqh.[74]

---

[71] Otto, *Sharia and National Law in Muslim Countries: Tensions and Opportunities for Dutch and Eu Foreign Policy.*
[72] Ibid.
[73] F. Robinson. *The Cambridge Illustrated History of the Islamic World.* Cambridge Illustrated Histories. Cambridge University Press, 1996. ISBN: 9780521669931.
[74] Badr, "Islamic Law: Its Relation to Other Legal Systems".

Most encyclopaedias define Sharia as law based upon the Qur'an, the Sunnah, and classical Fiqh derived from consensus (ijma) and analogy (qiyas). This definition of Sharia lumps together the revealed with the unrevealed. This blending of sources has created a muddled assumption that scholarly interpretations are as sacred and beyond revision as are the Qur'an and the Sunnah.

The Qur'an and the Sunnah constitute the immutable Basic Code, which should be kept separate from ever-evolving interpretive law (Fiqh). This analytical separation between the Basic Code and Fiqh is necessary to dissipate confusion around the term Sharia."[75]

Revival of the religion: Simultaneously with liberalizing and modernizing forces, trends towards fundamentalism and movements for Islamic political power are also taking place. There has been a growing religious revival in Islam, beginning in the eighteenth century and up to this present moment. This movement has expressed itself in various forms ranging from wars to efforts towards improving education.[76]

A return to traditional views of Sharia: There is a long-running worldwide movement underway by Muslims towards a better understanding and practice of their religion.

Encouraged by their scholars and imams, Muslims have moved away from local customs and culture, and towards more universally accepted views of Islam.

This is a movement away from or towards traditional religious values that served to help Muslims cope with the effects of European colonization. It also inspired modernist movements and the formation of new governments.[77]

---

[75]   A. Khan. "The Reopening of the Islamic Code: The Second Era of Ijtihad". eng. In: (2003).

[76]   Robinson, *The Cambridge Illustrated History of the Islamic World.*

[77]   Ibid.

The Islamist movement: Since the 1970s, the Islamist movements have become prominent; their goals are the establishment of Islamic states and Islamic Law within their own territories, and their approach is political in nature. Their rhetoric opposes Western culture and Western power.[78]

The Fundamentalist movement: Fundamentalists, desire to return to basic religious values and law, they have in some instances imposed harsh Sharia punishments for crimes, curtailed civil rights, and violated human rights. These movements are most active in areas of the world where there was contact with Western colonial powers.[79]

Extremism: Extremists have used the Qur'an and their own interpretation of the Islamic Law to justify acts of war and terror against Western individuals and governments, and also against other Muslims believed to have Western sympathies. Friction between the West and Islam, particularly with regard to the Palestinian issue, continues to fuel this conflict.[80]

---

[78]   Ibid.
[79]   Ibid.
[80]   Horrie and Chippindale, *What is Islam?: A Comprehensive Introduction.*

3. Islamic Judicial System and Governance

Man is a social being by nature. He cannot live perpetually on his own, completely independent of others. People are interdependent. Consequently, friction arises between them when their personal interests come into conflict with each other, or when what they perceive as their individual rights infringe upon those of others. Conflicts between them inevitably break out. In some cases, one party to the conflict might be strong and aggressive while the other is weak and condescending, incapable of defending his rights.

As a result of this, it becomes necessary to explore a way to prevent people from oppressing one another, to ensure that the weaker members of society receive justice, and to determine right from wrong when issues get complicated or uncertain. This can only be realized through a judge who has the authority to give legal verdicts in cases of dispute.

For this reason, we find that the existence of a judge is considered by Islamic Law and the laws of all the other revealed religions to be both a religious obligation and a necessity of human life.

Qur'an says:[1]

> We have sent Messengers with clear proofs, and sent down with them the Scripture and the Balance that mankind can establish justice. . . .
>
> - Qur'an 57:25

Islam – the religion that God wanted for mankind from the time that He sent Muhammad (PBUH), may the mercy and blessings of God be upon him until the Day of Judgment – shows great concern for the judicial system and those appointed to carry out its responsibilities.

Islam prescribes for it many legal injunctions. How else could it be, when Islam is the religion of mercy, equality, and justice? It is the religion that comes to free people from worshipping Creation and bring them to the worship of God. It is the religion that comes to remove people from oppression and iniquity; and bring them to the highest degree of justice and freedom.

God's Messenger was the greatest of all judges. He used to act in the capacity of the judge in the city of Medina, which was the first Islamic State. He used to appoint people to be judges in other cities. Among these were 'Utâb b. Asyad who was sent to Makkah, Ali b. Abu Talib and Muadh b. Jabal, both of whom were sent to Yemen.

In the era of the Rightly Guided Caliphs, the Head of State continued to be the one to appoint judges, govern their affairs, protect their independence, and keep the governors and political appointees – and even the Caliphs – subject to the judges' verdicts. Umar b. al-Khattaab, the second Caliph, was the first person to make the judge an independent entity, distinct from the Caliph and the governors.

In this way, the judicial system continued to evolve throughout the early Islamic era, during the Umayyad era, and well into the Abbasid era. The office of Chief Justice came into being at this time. The Chief Justice

---

[1]   *The Holy Qur'an (57:25).*

became responsible for appointing and removing judges. He was responsible for supervising their behaviour and monitoring their performance.

The first person to be appointed to this post was Justice Abu Yusuf, the student of the great jurist Abu Hanifah (may God have mercy on them both). Thereafter, this office became widespread throughout the Muslim lands. It continued to exist up to the fall of the Ottoman Empire.

The names of many just judges have been preserved in Islamic History. Their names are similitude to justice and integrity. Many pages in the history books are devoted to the lives and careers of eminent judges like Iyâs b. Muawiyah, Shurayh b. Abdallah, al-'Izz b. 'Abd al-Salam and others who applied the teachings of Islam in the best possible manner. They left a legacy on how a Muslim judge is supposed to conduct himself.

We should mention, since we are discussing the Islamic judicial system, that Islam sets down broad guidelines and basic principles concerning the affairs of life and rarely concerns itself with the particular details of life. This is so these guidelines can stay relevant for every time and place. One of these guidelines is the establishment of justice among people which is an obligation that has to be carried out.

As for the manner of achieving this objective, this has not been detailed in the sacred texts. This has been left for the people of each generation to deal with in a way most suited to their unique set of circumstances. The only condition is that whatever methods are chosen must not run contrary to Islamic Law.

3.1 The Uniqueness of Islamic Justice System

The judicial system in Islam is a system for deciding between people in litigation aiming at settling their disputes in accordance with the injunctions of the divine law, injunctions that are taken from the Qur'an and Sunnah.

All of the Messengers of God (praise of God be with them all) acted as judges.

Qur'an says:[2]

> And remember David and Solomon, when they gave judgment concerning the field when people's sheep had browsed therein at night, and We were witness to their judgment. And We made Solomon to understand the case. And to each of them, We gave good judgment and knowledge.
>
> - Qur'an 21:78-79

Qur'an also says:[3]

> O David, verily we have placed you as a successor on Earth, so judge between people in truth, and do not follow your desires for it will mislead you from the path of God. Verily, those who stray from the path of God have a severe punishment because they forgot the day of reckoning.
>
> - Qur'an 38:26

Prophet Muhammad (PBUH), who came with the final and eternal Message, was ordered by God to pass judgment in disputes just as he was ordered to spread the word of God and call people to Islam. This is mentioned in the Qur'an in a number of places.

Qur'an says:[4]

> So judge (O Muhammad (PBUH)) between them by what God has revealed and do not follow their vain desires, but beware of them lest they turn you away from some of what God has sent down to you.
>
> - Qur'an 5:49

---

[2]   *The Holy Qur'an (21:78-79).*
[3]   *The Holy Qur'an (38:26).*
[4]   *The Holy Qur'an (5:49).*

Qur'an also says:[5]

> "... And if you judge (O Muhammad (PBUH)), judge between them with justice. Verily, God loves those who act justly.
>
> - Qur'an 5:42

Qur'an says:[6]

> But no, by your Lord, they shall have no faith until they make you (O Muhammad (PBUH)) judge in all their disputes and find in themselves no resistance against your decisions and accept them with full submission.
>
> - Qur'an 4:65

The Sunnah also provides for the legal basis of the Islamic judicial system. It is related by Amr b. al-Aas that the Prophet said:[7]

> If a judge gives a judgment using his best judgment and is correct, then he receives a double reward (from God). If he uses his best judgment but makes a mistake, then he receives a single reward.
>
> - Ahmed

---

5   *The Holy Qur'an (5:42).*
6   *The Holy Qur'an (4:65).*
7   *Ahmed.* scholars.

God's Messenger said:[8]

> You should not wish to be like other people, except in two cases: a man who God has given wealth and he spends it on Truth and another who God has granted wisdom and he gives verdicts on its basis and teaches others.
>
> - Hadith (Sahih Al-Bukhari, Sahih Muslim)

Many scholars have related to us that there is consensus among Muslims on the legal status of the judicial system in Islam. Ibn Qudamah says:

> "The Muslims unanimously agreed that a judicial system must be established for the people."
>
> – Qudamah

3.1.1 Equality before the Law

Basically, Islam's rulings concerning civil rights do not differ from its rulings concerning the aforementioned equality rights. Islam treats all people equally before the law and grants them equal civil rights without any discrimination between a beggar and a prince, or a nobleman and a man of modest birth.

The Second Rightly Guided Caliph, 'Umar bin Al Khattaab, who was responsible for organizing the administration of justice in the Muslim state upon the firm foundation of the Holy Quran and the Traditions of the Prophet, said in his first speech after becoming Caliph:

> "O people I swear by God that there is no man among you as powerful as he who is helpless until I restore his rights to him, and there is no man amongst you as helpless as he who is powerful until I restore what he had usurped to its rightful owner."
>
> Umar bin Al Khattaab

---

[8]   *Sahih Al-Bukhari, Sahih Muslim.* Hadith.

'Umar bin Al Khattaab's message to Abu Musa Al Ash'ary concerning the administration of justice embodied the greater part of the rulings of the Faith of Islam on justice. He wrote "From the servant of God, 'Umar bin Al Khattaab, Commander of the Faithful, to the servant of God, Ibn Qais, (Peace be upon you).

> "The administration of justice is a religious duty and a tradition from the Prophet to be observed, so understand thoroughly the cases presented before you and enforce the sentence that you know to be just, for declaring the truth without executing justice is not just. Treat all people who stand before you equally in the way you greet them, address them and judge them. By so doing no nobleman would expect or hope for an unjust sentence in his favour and no poor man would despair of your just ruling."
>
> Umar bin Al Khattaab

Umar bin Al Khattaab last testament to his successor as Caliph was:

> "Treat all people equally and do not be influenced by any person who deserves punishment, and take no notice of any person's censure provided you have pronounced a just sentence. Never allow your preference or partiality for any person to influence your judgement in the affairs of the people whom God has entrusted to our authority."
>
> Umar bin Al Khattaab

The matter of equality in Islam was not limited to merely declaring principles and establishing laws, but history records that these principles and laws were executed solemnly and conscientiously during the lifetime of the Prophet Muhammad (PBUH), blessings and peace be upon him, and during the reign of the Four Rightly Guided Caliphs who succeeded him.

During the Golden Age of Islam which represents the principles and spirit of Islam in every respect Usama ibn Zayd, one of the most beloved companions of the Prophet Muhammad (PBUH), prayer and peace be upon him, once attempted to intercede with him on behalf of Fatima daughter of

Al Aswad Al Makhzoumiya who had been sentenced to the punishment of theft for stealing velvet material and golden ornaments.

The Prophet, blessings and peace be upon him, refused Osama's intercession, in spite of his affection for him and reprimanded him severely saying:

> "How can you intercede with me concerning a penalty ordained by God Almighty Allah." Then he said to the people who had witnessed the matter."
>
> Prophet Muhammad (PBUH)

Before the advent of Islam, people of noble descent were not punished if they were guilty of theft and poor indigent people were punished for the same crime.

> "I swear by God Almighty, that if my daughter Fatima were guilty of the crime of theft, I would sentence her to the punishment ordained by God Almighty."
>
> Prophet Muhammad (PBUH)

A Jew once lodged a complaint to the Caliph 'Umar bin Al Khattaab against 'Ali bin Abu Talib. When they both stood before the Caliph 'Omar, he addressed the Jew by his name and addressed 'Ali Abu Talib by his appellation of Abu Al Hasan (the Father of Hasan) as he was accustomed to addressing him. 'Ali showed signs of displeasure and the Caliph 'Umar asked him if he had resented his adversary being a Jew with whom he had been obliged to stand on equal footing before the Caliph.

'Ali ibn Abu Talib replied; that had not been the cause of his displeasure, the reason being that the Caliph had addressed the Jew by his name whereas he had addressed him by his appellation of Abu Al Hasan, which is a sign of respect and veneration. 'Ali bin Abu Talib had thus expressed his displeasure because 'Umar bin Al Khattaab had inadvertently treated him with more respect than his adversary.

A son of 'Amr bin Al 'Aas, the governor of Egypt, once struck a man of the lower class. The man swore that he would lodge a complaint to the Caliph 'Umar bin Al Khattab. 'Amr bin Al Aas's son told the man to do so, boasting that the Caliph would never punish him, since he was the son of the noble ruler of Egypt.

Later, during the pilgrimage season when the Caliph 'Umar, his entourage, 'Amr bin 'Al 'Aas, and his son were assembled together, the man whom 'Amr's son had struck went to the Caliph, and pointed to the son of 'Amr bin Al 'Aas and said: "This man struck me unjustly and when I threatened to complain to you, he told me that he was the son of a nobleman and that you would never punish him".

The Caliph 'Umar bin Al Khattab looked at 'Amr bin Al 'Aas and uttered his famous words "What right have you to enslave people, whose mothers gave birth to them as free people?" He then gave the man who had lodged his complaint a whip and told him to strike the son of the nobleman - namely the son of 'Amr bin Al 'Aas - as he had struck him.

On a certain occasion, the Caliph 'Umar witnessed a man and a woman committing adultery, so he assembled the people around him and said: "How should the Caliph of the Muslims act when he witnesses the sin of adultery being committed?"

'Ali bin Abu Talib replied: "There must be four witnesses to the sin of adultery and if he cannot present these witnesses and he accuses the man and woman of adultery, he must be punished for the sin of slander without sufficient evidence, as any other person would be punished in a similar situation". 'Ali bin Abu Talib then recited the following Quranic verse:[9]

> But no, by your Lord, they shall have no faith until they make you (O Muhammad (PBUH)) judge in all their disputes and find in themselves no resistance against your decisions and accept them with full submission.
>
> - Qur'an 24:4

---

[9] *The Holy Qur'an (24:4).*

85

The Caliph 'Umar did not reply nor did he reveal the identity of the man and woman whom he had witnessed committing the sin of adultery.

Islam applies the principle of equality in its treatment of Muslims and non-Muslims. Islam ordains that non-Muslims living in a Muslim state or in a state under Muslim rule have the same rights and obligations as their fellow Muslims. They are subject to the Muslim laws of justice except in matters concerning their religion. Accordingly, their faith and beliefs are respected by the state and the community in which they live.

Another example of Islamic Justice

Allah created man to be His servant and to implement His way on earth. If humans distance themselves from this message, then they distance themselves from God's injunctions. That is why Islam has prepared its followers to follow this righteous instinct, it is a joy to our spirit to stand and think of the greatness of Islamic justice, and how fair Islamic law is to individuals and groups, rulers, and the ruled!

Let us visit one of Islam's greatest and brightest symbols of justice, Shurayh Al-Qaadhi (the judge), who narrates:

The Caliph 'Umar ibn Al-Khattaab bought a horse from a Bedouin, paid its price and rode off with it. However, after travelling a little distance, the Caliph noticed some kind of defect in the horse so he returned it to the seller, requesting him to take it back since it was defective. The man refused, telling the Caliph that the horse was perfectly healthy when it was sold to him. 'Umar told the man to choose a judge and the man suggested Shurayh bin Al-Haarith Al-Kindi whom 'Umar accepted.

After the judge listened to the Bedouin's testimony, he turned to 'Umar asking: "Was the horse normal and healthy when you bought it?" 'Umar replied: "Yes, it was." Shurayh then said: "Then keep what you bought or return it as you took." 'Umar looked at Shurayh in admiration saying: "Thus justice should be – statement, distinguishing words and fair justice… I give you the position of Chief Justice of Qufah, now known as 'Iraq".

This is Islamic justice, an ordinary Bedouin taking the Caliph to court, deciding which judge to go to and the Caliph accepting the judge's decision voluntarily. However, this leader was not an ordinary man but the one about whom the Prophet (SAW), said: "O Allah! Make Islam victorious by one of the two 'Umars' (becoming Muslim)".

'Umar did not threaten the Bedouin or misuse his power, neither did he tell the Bedouin that he had exceeded his authority nor that he would get back to him. No, 'Umar accepted the judge's decision with all modesty.

'Umar admitted that the horse was healthy when he took it and he accepted the judgment, making the case an everlasting example of Islamic justice. The judge's fairness made 'Umar appoint him as a judge of Qufah. He rewarded the judge for his justice and fairness and did not jail him for ruling against him, as some leaders may have done in present so-called 'democracies'.

3.2 The Islamic Ruling Concerning the Judiciary

The jurists agree that the duty of the judge is an obligation that must be carried out by society. If some members of society carry out this duty, it is sufficient for everyone. If, on the other hand, everyone neglects it, then everyone in society is sinful.

The proof that this duty is obligatory comes from the Qur'an:[10]

> O you who believe! Stand out firmly for justice · · · · .
>
> - Qur'an 4:135

It is only necessary for a small number of individuals to perform judicial duties since judicial dispositions come under the broad duty of enjoining what is right and forbidding what is wrong. It is not obligatory

---

[10] *The Holy Qur'an (4:135).*

for every individual to carry out these duties as long as some people are doing so.

The affairs of the people will not be correct and upright without a judicial system. It is, consequently, obligatory for one to exist, just like it is necessary to have a military. Imam Ahmad, one of the greatest and most well-known scholars of Islam said:

"People have to have a judicial authority or their rights will disappear."

– Prophet Muhammad (PBUH)

The duties of the judiciary include enjoining what is right, helping the oppressed, securing people's rights, and keeping oppressive behaviour in check. None of these duties can be performed without the appointment of a judiciary.

A judicial system is a child of necessity for the prosperity and development of nations. It is needed to secure human happiness, protect the rights of the oppressed, and restrain the oppressor. It is the way to resolve disputes and ensure human rights. It serves as a catalyst to institute what is right, forbidding what is wrong, and curbing immoral behaviour.

In this way, a just social order can be enjoyed by all sectors of society, and every individual can feel secure in his life, property, honour, and liberty. In this environment, nations can progress, civilization can be achieved and people are free to pursue what will enhance them both spiritually and materially.

3.3 Legal Precedents under Islamic Law

Islamic judicial proceedings have significant differences with other legal traditions, including those in both common law and civil law. Islamic courts traditionally do not rely on lawyers; plaintiffs and defendants represent themselves. Trials are conducted solely by the judge, and there is no jury system (as is found in civil law in countries such as Russia and France).

Unlike common law, judges' verdicts do not set binding precedents[11] under the principle of stare decisis as established in the case of, *Saudi Arabia Basic Industries Corp. v. Mobil Yanbu Petrochemical Co.(2005),* Supreme Court of Delaware, found that: "The Saudi law system differs in critically important respects from the system of legal thought employed by the common law countries.

Perhaps most significant is that Islamic law does not embrace the common law system of binding precedent and stare decisis. Indeed, in Saudi Arabia, judicial decisions are not in themselves a source of law except with minor exceptions.

There are three categories of crimes in Islamic Law: *Qisas*, *Hudud*, and *Tazir*.

Qisas

Qisas involves personal injury and has several categories: intentional murder (first-degree), quasi-intentional murder (second-degree), unintentional murder (manslaughter), intentional battery, and unintentional battery.

A Qisas offense is treated as a civil case rather than an actual criminal case. If the accused party is found guilty, the victim (or in death, the victim's family) determines the punishment, choosing either retribution (Qisas-e-nafs), which means execution in the case of intentional murder, imprisonment, and in some cases of intentional battery, the amputation of the limb that was lost; or compensation (Diyya) for the loss of life/limb/injury.

The Islamic Law judge, thus in modern Islamic Law states like Iran or Iraq, the state can convict for and legally punish only Qisas crimes on his own authority. However, the state itself may prosecute for crimes committed alongside the Qisas offense.

If the victim's family pardons the criminal, in addition to the Sharia punishment he would normally receive a Tazir prison sentence (such as

---

[11] *Legal Literature And Institutions, Jurisprudence: The "sources" Of The Law, The Modern Period.* Islamic Law. Accessed July 9, 2023. JRank. URL: https://science.jrank.org/pages/7816/Law-Islamic.html# ixzz8fnRYTPrU.

10–20 years in prison) for crimes such as "intentional loss of life", "Tazir assault and battery" "disturbance of the peace", and so forth.

The second category of crimes is Hudud (or hadd). Hudud crimes are crimes whose penalties were laid down in the Qur'an, and are considered to be "crimes against God". Hudud crimes are adultery (zina): includes adultery, fornication, paedophilia, rape, and pimping; sodomy/lesbianism (or sodomy rape waging) war against God and society: armed robbery, terrorism, armed violence; theft; use of intoxicants (alcohol/drug use); apostasy/blasphemy; and defamation.

These cases are not meant as actual punishments, but as deterrents, and an example to the general public, and to prosecute the most flagrant violations. Hudud is meant as a deterrent, not a general punishment.

The process is extremely exacting, a minimum of two witnesses are required to corroborate the evidence, and in the case of sex crimes, four witnesses, thus making it in most cases hard, if not impossible, to receive the violent punishments. Circumstantial evidence is not allowed to be part of the testimony. When one does receive them, it usually would occur in a case where the offense was so obvious, obscene, or flagrant that it is impossible not to be convicted.

As a result, most countries do not prosecute Hudud offenses (the exceptions being Saudi Arabia and Afghanistan under the Taliban, which regularly managed to prosecute offenses in the Hudud category) almost all other countries, such as Iran, would usually punish the same offense as a Tazir crime.

The third category of crimes is *Tazir*. It covers all other offenses not mentioned already. It is a "claim of the state" and it receives a discretionary sentence. The punishment may not be more severe than the punishment of a Hudud crime.

It can range, depending on the crime or circumstances, from death to imprisonment to even community service. Circumstantial evidence is allowed, and most countries prosecute their crimes as Tazir crimes, due to the flexibility of the evidence-gathering and sentencing.

The punishment is meant to fit the crime. For example, a rapist may not be able to be prosecuted for zina, but would still be convicted of Tazir rape, or in theft, they would be found guilty of Tazir theft and given prison time rather than amputation. A murderer would still spend time in prison if he had received the forgiveness of the family. The heavy Hudud penalties of amputation and stoning are not applied (although some countries do use corporal punishment). Most modern countries such as Iran have a fixed penal code that regulates what sentences should be given depending on the crime and circumstances of the case.

Islamic Law courts' rules of evidence also maintain a distinctive custom of prioritizing oral testimony.[12] A confession, an oath, or the oral testimony of a witness is the main evidence admissible in a Hudud case, written evidence is only admissible when deemed reliable by the judge.

Testimony must be from at least two witnesses, and preferably free Muslim male witnesses, who are not related parties and who are of sound mind and reliable character; testimony to establish the crime of adultery, or zina must be from four direct witnesses.[13]

Forensic evidence (i.e. fingerprints, ballistics, blood samples, DNA, etc.) and other circumstantial evidence is not often used in Hudud cases rather eyewitnesses are relied upon, a practice which can cause severe difficulties for women plaintiffs in rape cases[14].[15] Testimony from women is given only half the weight of men, and non-Muslim minorities, could and did use Islamic Law courts, even amongst themselves.[16]

---

[12] **HammoudHassanR.**

[13] A. Ajijola. *Introduction to Islamic Law*. Adam Publishers & Distributors, 2007. ISBN: 9788174354266.

[14] Kamali. "Punishment in Islamic Law: a Critique of The Hudud Bill of Kelantan, Malaysia". In: *Arab Law Quarterly* 13 (1998), pp. 203–234. URL: https://api.semanticscholar.org/CorpusID:53065591.

[15] M. Kamali. *Punishment in Islamic Law: An Enquiry Into the Hudud Bill of Kelantan*. Ilmiah Publisher, 2000. ISBN: 9789832092285.

[16] T. Kuran. "Why the Middle East is Economically Underdeveloped: Historical Mechanisms of Institutional Stagnation". In: *Journal of Economic Perspectives* 18.3 (2004), 71–90. DOI: 10.1257/0895330042162421. URL: https://www.aeaweb.org/articles?id=10.1257/0895330042162421.

However, some of the reasons why non-Muslims used Islamic Law courts included more reliable enforcement, mandatory compliance, and the ability to switch between religious jurisdictions at any time, a privilege not available to Muslim litigants.

Essentially, written evidence, in the form of oaths is accorded much greater weight, rather than being used simply to guarantee the truth of ensuing testimony, the court may demand that defendants take an oath swearing their innocence; refusal thereof can result in a verdict for the plaintiff.[17]

Accordingly, defendants are not routinely required to swear before testifying, which would risk casually profaning the Qur'an should the defendant commit perjury,[18] instead oaths are a solemn procedure performed as a final part of the evidence process.

In some countries, Islamic Law courts, with their tradition of *pro se* representation, simple rules of evidence, and absence of appeals courts, prosecutors, cross-examination, complex documentary evidence and discovery proceedings, juries and voir dire proceedings, circumstantial evidence, forensics, case law, standardized codes, exclusionary rules and most of the other infrastructures of civil and common law court systems, have as a result, comparatively informal and streamlined proceedings.

This can provide significant increases in speed and efficiency; and can be an advantage in jurisdictions where the general court system is slow or corrupt and where few litigants can afford lawyers.

In Nigeria, where implementation of Islamic Law was highly controversial, even Nigeria's justice minister admitted that in Islamic Law courts, "if a man is indebted to you, you can get paid in the evening.

---

[17]   M. Lippman, S. McConville, and M. Yerushalmi. *Islamic Criminal Law and Procedure: An Introduction*. Bloomsbury Academic, 1988. ISBN: 9780275930097.

[18]   M. J. Frank. ""Trying Times: The Prosecution of Terrorists in the Central Criminal Court of Iraq". In: *Florida Journal of International Law* 18.1 (2006), 71–90. DOI: 10. 1257/ 0895330042162421. URL: https: //scholarship.law.ufl.edu/fjil/vol18/iss1/1.

Whereas in the regular courts, you can sit in court for ten years and get no justice.[19]"

Other systems, such as Iran, Iraq, and Pakistan, use a civil Islamic Law code similar to Western countries, and do have defence attorneys, prosecutors, and appeals courts. They also have a Supreme Court, and a definite civil law style penal code, but are still heavily based on the informality and simplicity of a "pure" Islamic Law court, and trials often still take a matter of hours or sometimes days.

3.4 Penalties

The punishment depends on whether the criminal was convicted of Qisas, Hudud, or Tazir. In a Tazir crime, the penalty would be usually a prison sentence, corporal punishment in some countries, or an execution in a more serious case (such as a case that was not prosecuted as Hudud, like rape/drug trafficking).

Since Hudud crimes are extremely hard to punish, this is the usual route that would be taken. Stoning and amputation would certainly not be carried out in a Tazir sentence, and the punishment would not be fixed, but discretionary. Most countries have a civil code that regulates the penalties that should be received in a Tazir crime, such as a death sentence in the case of drug trafficking, aggravated rape, or prison time in the case of other offenses.

In accordance with the Qur'an and several Hadith, theft is punished by imprisonment or amputation of hands.[20] Several requirements are in place for the amputation of hands, they are:

---

[19]   *The attractions of sharia: Nigeria's sharia courts are harsh, but quicker and cleaner than secular ones.* Islamic law in Nigeria. Accessed July 9, 2023. The Economist, 2002. URL: https://www.economist.com/middle-east-and-africa/2002/09/05/the-attractions-of-sharia.

[20]   *The Holy Qur'an (5:38).*

- There must have been criminal intent to take private (not common) property. The theft must not have been the product of hunger, necessity, or duress.
- The goods stolen must: be over a minimum value, not Haram, and not owned by the thief's family.
- Goods must have been taken from custody (i.e. not in a public place).
- There must be reliable witnesses.

All of these must be met under the scrutiny of judicial authority.[21]

In accordance with Hadith, stoning to death is the penalty for married men and women who commit adultery. In addition, there are several conditions related to the person who commits it that must be met[22],[23]

One of the difficult ones is that the punishment cannot be enforced unless there is a confession of the person involved or four male eyewitnesses, in which each of them saw the act being committed. All of these must be met under the scrutiny of judicial authority.[24]

For unmarried men and women, the punishment prescribed in the Qur'an and Hadith is 100 lashes[25][26],[27] The "four witness" standard comes from the Qur'an itself, a revelation in response to accusations of adultery levelled at Muhammad (PBUH)'s wife, Aisha:[28]

> Why did they not produce four witnesses? Since they produce not witnesses, they verily are liars in the sight of Allah.
>
> - Qur'an 24:13

---

[21]   Ibid.
[22]   *Sahih Al-Bukhari.* Hadith 8:82:815.
[23]   *Sahih Al-Bukhari.* Hadith 8:82:826.
[24]   B. Wikipedians. *Islam.* PediaPress.
[25]   Ibid.
[26]   *Sahih Al-Bukhari.* Hadith 8:82:818.
[27]   *The Holy Qur'an (24:2).*
[28]   *The Holy Qur'an (24:13).*

Punishments are authorized by other passages in the Qur'an and Hadith for certain crimes (e.g., extramarital sex, adultery), and are employed by some as the rationale for extra-legal punitive action while others disagree:[29][30]

> The woman and the man guilty of adultery or fornication—flog each of them with hundred stripes: Let no compassion move you in their case, in a matter prescribed by God, if ye believe in God and the last day.
>
> - Qur'an 24:2

> Nor come nigh to adultery: for it is a shameful (deed) and an evil, opening the road (to other evils).
>
> - Qur'an 17:32

Leaving Islam/Apostasy

In most interpretations of Sharia, conversion by Muslims to other religions or becoming non-religious is strictly not encouraged and is sometimes termed apostasy. Non-Muslims, however, are allowed to convert to Islam at their own free will.[31] Muslim theology equates apostasy to treason, and in most interpretations of Islamic Law, the penalty for apostasy is death.

However, nowadays, many scholars differentiate between treason and apostasy, believing that the punishment for apostasy is not death, while the punishment for treason is death.

---

[29] *The Holy Qur'an (24:2)*.

[30] *The Holy Qur'an (17:32)*.

[31] *2022 Report on International Religious Freedom: Malaysia*. Report. Accessed July 9, 2024. U.S. Department of State, 2022. URL: https://www.state.gov/reports/2022-report-on-international-religious-freedom/malaysia/#:~:text=A%20non-Muslim%20wishing%20to,faith%20without%20explicit%20parental%20permission..

The accusation of apostasy may be used against non-conventional interpretations of the Qur'an. The severe persecution of the famous expert in Arabic literature, Nasr Abu Zayd, is an example of this.[32]

Dietary

Islamic law does not present a comprehensive list of pure foods and drinks, but rather, it prohibits the following:[33][34]

Swine, blood, the meat of dead animals, and animals slaughtered other than in the name of God. Slaughtering an animal in any other way except the prescribed manner of *tazkiyah* (cleansing) by taking God's name, which involves cutting the throat of the animal and draining the blood. Slaughtering with a blunt blade or physically ripping out the oesophagus is strictly forbidden.[35]

Modern methods of slaughter like the captive bolt stunning and electrocuting are also prohibited. Causing the animal excessive pain during slaughter is a sin.[36]

The prohibition of dead meat is not applicable to fish and locusts. Also, Hadith prohibits beasts having sharp canine teeth, birds having claws and talons in their feet, Jallalah (animals whose meat carries a stink in it because they feed on filth), tamed donkeys, and any piece cut from a living animal.[37]

Liquor and Gambling

Liquor and gambling are expressly prohibited in the Qur'an, and Islamic law. Muhammad (PBUH) is reported to have said:

---

[32] *The battle for a religion's heart.* Egypt and global Islam. Accessed July 9, 2023. The Economist, 2009. URL: https://www.economist.com/international/2009/08/06/the-battle-for-a-religions-heart.

[33] *Islamic dietary laws.* Article. Accessed July 9, 2024. Wikipedia, 2022. URL: https://en.wikipedia.org/wiki/Islamic_dietary_laws#:~:text=Forbidden%20food%20substances%20include%20alcohol,in% 20the%20name%20of%20God..

[34] N. Deuraseh. "Lawful and unlawful foods in Islamic law focus on Islamic medical and ethical aspects". In: 2009. URL: https://api.semanticscholar.org/CorpusID:37911332.

[35] Wikipedians, *Islam.*

[36] Al-Misri, *The Reliance of the Traveller (edited and translated by Nuh Ha Mim Keller).*

[37] Wikipedians, *Islam.*

"He who plays with dice is like the one who handles the flesh and blood of swine."

– Prophet Muhammad (PBUH)

Abd-Allah ibn Amr reported that Muhammad (PBUH) (SAW) prohibited all games of chance and card playing that caused financial gain or loss.[38]

3.5 Islamic Political System

The Islamic political system is based on three principles, which are: Tawheed (Oneness of God), Risalat (Prophethood), and Khilafat (Caliphate). The sovereignty of this kingdom depends only on Him-God. He alone has the right to command or forbid. Worship and obedience are due to Him alone, none else sharing it in any degree or form.

Life, in all its multifarious forms, human physical organs and reasoning, the apparent control which they have over everything that exists in this universe and the things themselves none of them has been created or acquired by mankind in its own right, rather they are the bountiful provisions of God which He bestowed upon mankind; no one is as Him (AT-TAWHEED).

Hence, it is neither for human beings to decide the aim and purpose of their existence or to prescribe the limits of worldly authority nor is anyone else entitled to make these decisions for mankind. This right vests only in God, who has created mankind, endowed mankind with mental and physical abilities; and provided all material provisions for the use of mankind.

This principle of the Oneness of God altogether negates the concept of the legal and political sovereignty of human beings, individually or collectively. Nothing can claim sovereignty, be it a human being, a family,

---

[38]   Ibid.

a class, or group of people, or even the human race in the world as a whole. God alone is the Sovereign and His commandments are the Laws of Islam.

The medium through which the Law is communicated is known as **"Risalat" (Prophethood)**. Hence, two things originated from this source:

The Book in which the Islamic Law has been expounded; and the authoritative interpretation and exemplification of the Qur'an by the Prophet, through his words and deeds, in his capacity as the last messenger of God which is the Sunnah.

Furthermore, the Prophet (SAW) has, in accordance with the intention of the divine book, set up for mankind a model of the system of life in Islam by practically implementing the law and providing necessary details where necessary. The combination of these two elements, according to Islamic terminology, is called the "Shari'ah" meaning Islamic Law. There is a specific purpose for man's existence. This purpose is achieved when man fulfils his function and is missed when a man fails to live up to his designated role and/or expectations.

However, this special role linking man to his Creator is subservience to Allah and worship of Him. All aspects of mankind's life are based on this consideration. Thus, the meaning of worship must be extended to go beyond mere rituals into all activities since Allah does not only call upon mankind to perform rituals but His injunctions regulate all aspects of life. The Qur'an states:[39]

> Behold, thy Lord said to the angels: 'I will create a vicegerent on earth' ·····.
>
> - Qur'an 2:30

Basically, it is the Khilafat (Caliphate) on earth that encompasses the range of activities of mankind. It consists of settlement on earth, exploration of its resources and energies, fulfilment of God's purpose of

---

[39]   *The Holy Qur'an (2:30).*

making full use of its resources, and developing life on it. In brief, this task requires the implementation of God's way which is in harmony with the divine law governing the whole universe. Thus, it becomes clear that the meaning of worship, which is the very purpose of man's existence and his primary function, is much more comprehensive than mere rituals. The role of Khilafat (Caliphate) is definitely an integral part of the meaning of worship. The truth about worship comes out in two essential points, namely:

- There should be a feeling of absolute certainty and conviction about the meaning of worship of God in one's heart; a feeling that the only possible relationship which holds is one's creator and the created and nothing but that.

- It is imperative to turn to Allah dedicating to Him every stir of one's conscience, every fluttering of the senses, every movement of life. This dedication should be channelled solely to Him and nobody else. No other feeling should have any room left, except in so far as it is construed as part of the meaning of worship of God. In this way, the meaning of worship is fulfilled. Thus, work becomes one with rituals; rituals one with settlement on earth; like striving for God's cause; striving in the way of God which incorporates patience in bearing calamities contentedly in the knowledge that they are part of God's plan; all these are instances of worship of God.

With this healthy frame of mind, based on the right understanding of man's role in this universe, man becomes ready to implement God's teaching, as communicated through the message of Prophet Muhammad (PBUH).

This is exactly what Islam means when it lays down that man is Khalifah (vicegerent) of God on the earth. The state that is established in accordance with this political theory will have to fulfil the purpose and intent of God by working on God's earth within the limits prescribed by Him and in conformity with His instructions and injunctions.

3.5.1 Purpose of Islamic State

Islamic state is the type of state that is built on the foundation of Tawheed (the Oneness of God), "Risalat" (the Prophethood of Muhammad (PBUH)) and "Khilafat" (the Caliphate). The Holy Qur'an clearly states that the aim and purpose of this state is the establishment, maintenance, and development of those virtues, with which the creator of this universe wishes human life to be adorned and the prevention and eradication of those evils, the presence of which in human life is utterly abhorrent to God.

Hence, The state in Islam is not intended for political administration only nor the fulfilment through it of the collective will of any particular set of people; rather, Islam places a high ideal before the state for the achievement of which, it must use all the means at its disposal; and this purpose is that the qualities of purity, beauty, goodness, virtue, success, and prosperity which God wants to flourish in the life of His people, should be evolved.

Apparently, all kinds of exploitation, injustice, and disorders which, in the view of God, are ruinous for the world and detrimental to the life of His creatures are suppressed and prevented. Simultaneously, Islam gives a clear outline of its moral system clearly stating the desired virtues and the undesirable evils. Keeping this outline in view, the Islamic State can plan its welfare program at every age and in any environment.

The persistent demand made by Islam is that it lays down an unalterable policy for the state to base its politics on justice, truth and honesty. It is not prepared, under any circumstance whatsoever, to tolerate fraud, falsehood and injustice for the sake of any political, administrative, or national expediency. Whether it is the mutual relations of the rulers and the ruled within the state, or the relations of the state with other states, precedence must always be given to truth, honesty, and justice over material consideration.

Thus, It imposes similar obligations on the state as well as on the individual, to fulfil all contracts and obligations, to have uniform measures and standards for dealings, to remember duties along with the rights and not to forget the rights of other when expecting them to fulfil their obligations; to use power and authority for the establishment of justice and not for the perpetration of injustice; to look upon duty as a sacred obligation and to fulfil it scrupulously; and to regard power as a trust from God and use it with the belief that one has to render an account of one's actions to Him in the Hereafter.

3.5.2 Human Rights and Islamic Law

Fundamentally, an Islamic state may be set up in any portion of the earth; Islam does not seek to restrict human rights or privileges to the geographical limits of its own state. Islam has laid down some universal fundamental rights for humanity as a whole, which are to be observed and respected under all circumstances whether such a person is resident within the territory of the Islamic state or outside it, whether he is at peace with the state or at war.

Human blood is sacred in any case and cannot be spilled without justification which is equivalent to the 'right to life' under the Human Rights Act 1998. It is not permissible to oppress women, children, old people, sick persons, or the wounded. Woman's honour and chastity are worthy of respect under all circumstances.

The hungry person must be fed, the naked must be clothed, and the wounded treated medically irrespective of whether they belong to the Islamic community or not and/or even if they are from amongst its enemies. These and a few other provisions laid down by Islamic fundamental rights for every man by virtue of his status as a human being are designed to be enjoyed under the constitution of an Islamic state.

Hence, the rights of citizenship in Islam are not confined to persons born within the limits of its state but are granted to every Muslim irrespective of his place of birth. A Muslim ipso facto becomes a citizen of an Islamic state as soon as he sets his foot on its territory with the intent to live therein and thus enjoys equal rights of citizenship along with those who acquire its citizenship by birth.

Citizenship has therefore been common among all the Islamic states that may exist in the world and a Muslim will not need any passport for entry into or exit from any of them. And every Muslim is to be regarded as eligible and fit for all positions of the highest responsibility in an Islamic State without any discussions of race colour or class. Islam has also laid down certain rights for the non-Muslims who may be living within the boundaries of an Islamic State and these rights must necessarily form part of the Islamic Constitution.

According to the Islamic terminology such non-Muslims are Dhimmee meaning the covenant. This implies that the Islamic State has entered into a covenant with them and guaranteed their protection.

Their life and property are protected exactly like that of a Muslim citizen. There is no difference at all between a Muslim and a Dhimmee with respect to civil or criminal law. The Islamic State shall not interfere with the personal law of the Dhimmee. They will have full freedom of conscience and belief.

3.5.3 Executive and the Legislative

The responsibility for the administration of the Government, in an Islamic state, is entrusted to an Amir (leader or chief) who may be likened to the President or the Prime Minister in a conventional democratic state. The basic qualifications for the election of an Amir are that he should command the confidence of the ABLUL HAL WAL'AQD [The Constitutional Body).

They are recruited from among the scholars (of Islam), leaders, and notables who effectively have the duty to carry out this task of appointing the ruler. In this, they do not act on their own personal preferences, but on behalf of the whole nation, being as they are, its representatives. Three conditions must be met for eligibility to membership of this body, namely:

- Piety and morally sound.

- To be well versed in religion so as to be in a position to decide upon who deserves the position of Amir.

- Good and sound judgment leads to a sharp perception of who is most suitable for the role of Amir.

The Amir can retain office only so long as he observes God's law. Being himself the primary example of it both in his dealings and conduct, honouring his commitments and being true to his trust; in brief, he should conform to the conditions originally stipulated upon his holding office and will have to vacate his office when he loses this confidence. But as long as he retains such confidence he will have the authority to govern and exercise the powers of the government, in consultation with the Shura (the advisory council) and within the limits set by the Islamic Law. However, every citizen has the right to criticize the Amir should he deviate from the straight path, fail to honour the trust laid in him, transgress and tyrannize over people, change his conduct for the worst, freeze the implementation of God's penal code, or flouts God's regulations in any way. If he fails to live up to one of the conditions stipulated for his eligibility to the office, the nation has the right to overrule his judgment either by correcting him or by deposing them.

Legislation in an Islamic state is restricted within the limits prescribed by Islamic Law; the injunctions of God and the legislative body cannot make any alterations or modifications in them or make any law repugnant to them. As for the commandments that are liable to two or more interpretations, the duty of ascertaining the real intent of the Islamic judicial system, in such cases, will devolve on people possessing specialized knowledge of the law of the Islamic judicial system. Hence, such affairs will have to be referred to a subcommittee of the advisory council compressing men learned in Islamic Law. A vast field will still be available for legislation on questions not covered by any specific injunctions of the Islamic judicial system and the advisory council or legislature will be free to legislate in regard to these matters.

In Islam, the **judiciary** is not placed under the control of the executive. It derives its authority directly from the Islamic judicial system (Shari'ah) and is answerable to God. The judges, no doubt can be appointed by the Government but once a judge has occupied the bench he will have to administer justice among the people according to the law of God in an impartial manner.

The organs and functionaries of the Government will not be outside his legal jurisdiction much so that even the highest executive authority of the Government is liable to be called upon to appear in a court of law as a plaintiff or defendant like any other citizen of the state.

Rulers and the ruled are subject to the same law and there can be no discrimination on the basis of position, power or privilege. Islam stands for equality and scrupulously sticks to this principle in social, economic and political realms alike.

3.6 Socio-Economic Principles in Islam

Islam has laid down some principles and prescribed certain limits for the economic activities of humanity, so that the entire pattern of production, exchange, and distribution of wealth may conform to the Islamic standard of justice and equity. Islam does not concern itself with time-bound methods and techniques of economic production with the details of the pattern and mechanisms, organizational pattern, or equity.

Such methods are specific for every age and are evolved in accordance with the needs and requirements of the community and the exigencies of the economic situation. What Islam aims at, is that whatever the form or mechanism of economic activity, the principles prescribed by it should find a permanent and paramount place in such activities under all circumstances and in all ages.

According to the Islamic point of view, God has created for mankind the earth and all that it contains. It is, therefore, the birthright of every human being to try and secure his share of the world. All men enjoy this right equally and none can be deprived of it nor should one man get precedence over another.

In addition, from the standpoint of Islam, there can be no bar on any individual, race, or class for taking to certain means of livelihood or adopting certain professions. All are entitled to equal opportunities in the economic realm.

Similarly, no distinction is valid in Islam which would result in creating a monopoly of a particular means of livelihood for a particular person, class, race or group of people. It is the right of all men to strive and get their share of the means of sustenance provided by God on the earth. Islam ensures that this effort should be made in the context of equal opportunities and fair chances for all.

3.6.1 Proprietary Right in Property

Resources that are provided by nature free of cost and which can be used directly by man may be utilized freely and everyone is entitled to benefit from them to the extent of his needs.

Water flowing in the rivers and springs, woods in the forest trees, fruits of wild plants, wild grass and fodder, air, animals of the jungle, minerals under the surface of the earth and similar other resources cannot be monopolized by anyone nor can a restriction of any sort be imposed on their free use by God's creatures to fulfil their own needs.

In a real sense, people who may want to use any of these things for commercial purposes can be required to pay taxes to the state or if there is a misuse of the resources, the Government may step in and set the things right. However, there is no bar on the individuals to avail of God's earth as long as they do not interfere with the rights of others or of the state.

Anyone who takes possession of the natural resources directly and renders them of value acquires a rightful title over them. For instance, if somebody takes possession of an uncultivated piece of land, on which nobody has a prior right of ownership, and makes a productive use of it, he cannot be arbitrarily dispossessed of that piece of land.

This is how rights of ownership originated in the world. When a man appeared for the first time in the world and the population grew, everything was available to everyone. And whoever took possession of anything and made it useful in any manner became its owner; that is to say, he acquired the right to use it specifically for his own purpose and obtained compensation from others if they wanted to use it.

This is the natural basis of all the economic activities of mankind and must not be tampered with. This right of ownership which one may acquire by permissible legal means is to be honoured under all circumstances.

The legality of ownership can be inquired thoroughly by the competent authority through legal means to determine its validity in accordance with Islamic Law. If it is found to be illegally acquired, such ownership be annulled and be terminated accordingly. However, in no case, shall there be allowed any state or legislation to arbitrarily divest the people of their legitimate rights of ownership without justifiable cause.

Islam would not approve of an economic policy that destroys the rights conferred by the Islamic judicial system. However, attractive its name may be and whatever welfare pretensions it may make. Social justice and collective good are very dear to Islam, but not at the cost of rights accorded by Islamic Law.

It is as unjust to reduce or remove the restrictions placed by Islamic Law on the rights of individual ownership for the sake of the collective good of the community as it is to add such restrictions and limitations which do not fit into the scheme of the Islamic law.

It is one of the duties of an Islamic state to protect the legal rights of individuals and to ensure that they fulfil their obligations to the community as enjoined by the law, by which Islam strikes a balance between individualism and collectivism.

3.6.2 The Problem of Equity

If we observe the phenomena of nature and God's blessings unto mankind, we find that He has not observed equality in the distribution of His bounties and favours but in His infinite wisdom has accorded precedence to some individuals over others. The beauty of form, pleasantness of voice, excellence of physique and mental talents, etc, have not been granted to men in equal degree. The same is the case with the material means of life.

Human nature has been so ordained that divergence, variety and inequality among men in their modes and standards of living seem to be the most natural thing. Variety is the spice of life and the driving spirit behind human effort and excellence.

Consequently, all those schemes and ideologies which are forced on mankind are unrealistic and impossible to achieve. The equality in which Islam believes is equality in respect of the opportunities of struggle for securing a livelihood and for climbing the uppermost rung of the ladder of well-being and prosperity.

Islam desires that no legal, functional, or traditional handicaps should exist in society, to prevent an individual from struggling for a living according to his capacity and talent nor should any social distinctions subsist with the object of safeguarding the privileges of a particular class, race and dynasty or group of people, as well as those schemes and ideologies which serve the vested interests or which want to perpetrate the hold of a certain group are repugnant to Islam and can have no place in its scheme of things.

Such movements seek to establish, through force and resort to artificial means, an unnatural inequality in place of the natural limited inequality that feeds the springs of incentive to effort in society.

Hence, Islam aims to wipe them out and put the economic system on a natural footing so that the opportunities of struggle may remain open to all. At the same time, Islam does not agree with those who desire to enforce complete equality in respect of the means of production and the fruits of economic endeavour, as they aim at replacing, limited natural inequalities with artificial equality.

Only that system can be the nearest to human nature in which everyone joins the economic struggle at the start and in the circumstances in which God has created him. He, who has inherited an airplane, should struggle to be equipped with it; while he who has only a pair of legs should stand on his feet and try to move ahead.

The laws of society should neither establish a permanent monopoly of the airplane owner over his airplane nor make it impossible for the bare-footed to acquire an airplane nor such that the race for every one of them should compulsorily begin from one point. And under the same conditions and they should all perforce be tied to each other right till the end of the race.

Contrary to this, the economic laws should be such as to make it possible for the bare-footed who started his race under adverse conditions, to secure and possess an airplane if he can do so by dint of his struggle and ability. And for him who inherited the airplane, to be left behind in the race and be without it if that is due to his own inability or incapacity or inefficiency. Effort should be paid and inactivity penalized.

3.6.3 Social Justice

Islam does not wish for its economic race to take place in an atmosphere of cold impartiality, moral neutrality, and social apathy. It deems it desirable that the participants in the economic race should be considerate and sympathetic to one another.

On the one hand, Islam through its moral injunctions aims at creating a feeling of mutual love and affection among the people, under which they may help their weak and weary brethren and at the same time create a permanent institution in the society, to guarantee help and assistance to those who are lacking in the necessary means of subsistence.

People, who are unable to take part in the economic race, should secure their share from this social institution. And those who need some assistance commence their struggle in the economic field and may also receive it in full measure from this institution. To this end, Islam has commanded that Zakat should be levied at the rate of 2.5 percent per annum on the total accumulated wealth of the country as well as on the invested capital.

On agricultural produce, 10% is levied on lands that are irrigated by natural means (through rains) and 5 percent on irrigation which requires man's efforts while 2.5 percent is required on mineral products. The annual Zakat should also be levied at a specified rate, on the herds of cattle owned by anyone beyond a certain minimum number. The amount of Zakat thus collected is to be spent on giving assistance to the poor, the orphans, the indigent, etc.

This provides a means of social insurance in the presence of which no one in an Islamic society can ever remain without being well provided with the necessities of life. No worker can ever be forced to accept any conditions of employment which may be dictated to him by the industrialist or the landlord to his disadvantage. And nobody's physical health can ever be allowed to fail below the minimum standard of fitness for lack of proper medical care and hospitalization.

With regards to the position of the individual, in relation to the community, Islam aims at striking a balance between both as it would promote the individual liberty of a person and at the same time ensure that such freedom is not detrimental to the interests of the community as a whole.

Rather it is positively conducive to its growth and tranquillity. Islam does not approve of a political or economic organization that aims at merging the identity of the individual into that of the community and depriving him of the freedom essential for the proper development of his personality and talent.

The inevitable consequence of nationalizing all the means of production in a country is the annihilation of the individual by the community, and in these circumstances, the existence and development of his individuality becomes extremely difficult, if not impossible.

Fundamentally, just as political and social freedom is essential for the individual, economic freedom is likewise essential for a civilized moral existence. Unless we desire to completely eliminate the individuality of man, our social life should have enough margins for an individual to have the freedom to earn his living, to maintain the freedom of his conscience, to be able to develop his moral and intellectual faculties according to his own inclinations and aptitudes.

Even though, Islam does not favour a social system that gives unbridled economic and social freedom to individuals and gives them a blank check to secure their individual interests and achieve their objective of exploiting and misappropriating the wealth of others.

Islam rather adopted the middle course by which the individual is first called upon, in the interest of the community, to accept certain restrictions and is then left free to regulate his own affairs. He has freedom of enterprise and competition within a framework that safeguards the interests of both the individual and the society.

3.6.4 Obligations and Restrictions

The meticulous care with which Islam has distinguished between right and wrong with respect to the means of earning wealth is not to be found in any other legal and social system existing in the world. It condemns as illegal all those means of livelihood that injure, morally or materially, the interests of another individual or of the society as a whole.

Islamic law categorically rejects and categorises as illegal the manufacture and sale of liquor and other intoxication, adultery, professional dancing and obscenity, gambling, speculation, race and lotteries, transactions of speculative, imaginary, fraudulent, or controversial nature; business transactions in which the gain of one party is absolutely guaranteed and assured while that of the other party is left uncertain and doubtful; price manipulation by withholding the sale of necessities of life; and many other similar transactions which are detrimental to the interests of the community.

On examining this aspect of the economic laws of Islam, we will find a long list of practices declared illegal most of which can and are making people millionaires in the capitalistic system. Islam forbids all these unfair means and allows freedom of earning wealth only by those means through which a person renders some real and useful service to the community and thereby entitles him to a fair and just compensation for it.

Islam accepts the rights of ownership of an individual the rights of ownership of an individual over the wealth earned by him by legitimate means but even these rights are not unqualified.

A man can spend his legitimate wealth, only in legitimate avenues and by legitimate means. Islam has imposed restrictions on expenditure so that while one can lead a decent life, one cannot waste one's riches on luxurious pursuits.

Certain forms of illegal and wasteful expenditure have been clearly and unequivocally prohibited while some others, though not expressly banned, may be prohibited at the discretion of the Islamic State.

One is permitted to accumulate wealth that is left over after meeting his legitimate and reasonable requirements, and these savings can also be used to produce more wealth but there are some restrictions on both of these activities. In the event of accumulation of wealth he will, of course, have to pay Zakat at the rate of 2.5% per annum on the accumulation exceeding the specified minimum.

If he desires to invest it in business, he can only do so in what is declared as legitimate business. It is permissible for a man to undertake the legitimate business himself or to make his capital available to others on a profit/loss sharing basis.

It is not objectionable in Islam if, working by making capital available as stated above enables a man to become a millionaire, rather, in the interests of the community as a whole Islam imposes two conditions on the individual:

- Firstly, that he should pay Zakat on his commercial goods and 'Ushr (1/10) (which has not required any man's effort for irrigation) and 5 percent on irrigated produce which has required man's efforts of the value of agricultural produce,
- Secondly, that he should deal fairly and honestly with those whom he brings into his partnership in the trade industry or agriculture, with those whom he takes in his employment, with the state and the community at large. If one does not do justice to others, particularly his employees, of his own accord, the Islamic State will compel him to do so.

Then again, even wealth that is accumulated within these legal limits is not allowed by Islam to be concentrated at a point or place for a long time. By virtue of inheritance, Islam spreads it over a large number of persons from generation to generation. In this respect, the spirit of Islamic law is different from that of other laws prevailing in the contemporary world. Most of the inheritance laws attempt to keep the wealth once accumulated by a person concentrated in the hands of the beneficiary from generation to generation.

As against this, Islam has made a law under which the wealth accumulated by a person in his lifetime is distributed among all of his close relatives soon after his death. If, there are no close relatives, then distant relatives are to benefit from it in the proportions laid down by the law for each one of them.

In addition, if no distant relative is forthcoming, then the entire Muslim society is entitled to its inheritance. Under this law, the creation or continuance of any big family of capitalists or landlords becomes impossible.

3.7 Islamic Law: A Legal System or Legal Tradition?

3.7.1 What Is Common In Islamic Law and Common Law?

Parallels to common law concepts are found in classical Islamic Law and Jurisprudence including *ratio decidendi (illah)*. Several fundamental common law institutions may have been adapted from similar legal institutions in Islamic Law and Jurisprudence, and introduced to England after the Norman conquest of England by the Normans, who conquered and inherited the Islamic legal administration of the Emirate of Sicily, and also by Crusaders during the Crusades.

In particular, the "Royal English contract protected by the action of debt is identified with the Islamic Aqd, the English assize of novel disseisin is identified with the Islamic Istihqaq, and the English jury is identified with the Islamic Lafif."

The English trust and agency institutions in common law were possibly adapted from the Islamic Waqf and Hawala institutions respectively during the Crusades. However, it is worth noting, that transferring property to another for the "use" of another developed largely in response to the requirements of feudal inheritance law.

Trust law, in particular, is a creature of equity derived from the parallel jurisdiction of the Lord Chancellor to decide matters independently to the Royal Courts.

Other English legal institutions such as "the scholastic method, the license to teach," the "law schools known as Inns of Court in England and Madrasas in Islam" and the "European commenda" (Islamic Qirad) may have also originated from Islamic law. The methodology of legal precedent and reasoning by analogy (Qiyas) are also similar in both the Islamic and common law systems. These similarities and influences have led some scholars to suggest that Islamic law laid the foundations for "the common law as an integrated whole".[40]

---

[40] **MoghulUmarF.**

3.7.2 A Comparative View of Fair Hearing/ Fair Trial under Common Law and the Islamic Law

Fair hearing is the fundamental Principle of natural Justice embraced within the concept of the rule of law i.e., fair hearing is the opportunity afforded to parties to proceedings to present their grievances with no obstruction from the authority.

This simply means the right of a party to a trial to present his evidence, to cross-examine witnesses called, and be appraised of the evidence against him, so that at the conclusion of the hearing, he may be in a position to know all the evidence on which the matter is to be decided. This principle equally applies to an accused person in criminal litigation.

Hence, Mr. Justice Blackburn in 1873 stated thus: ". . . None shall, by misrepresentation or otherwise, bring unfair pressure to bear on one of the parties to a cause so as to force him to drop his complaint, or to give up his defence, or to a settlement on terms which he would not otherwise have been prepared to entertain".

However, a hearing cannot be fair if any of the parties is refused a hearing or denied the opportunity to be heard, present his case or call witnesses. The principle of fair hearing is equated to fair trial as well as to natural Justice.

I believe it is an acceptable assumption, that the true test of a fair hearing in a case has always been the impression created in the mind of a reasonable person who was present at the trial, whether Justice has been done in the case or not. In order to achieve the principle of fair hearing, there are two inherent rules to be adhered to in all circumstances.

The first is the common law principle *Audi alteram partem* (or *audiatur et altera pars*) which is a Latin phrase that literally means "hear the other side" or "hear the alternative party". While the second principle is *Nemo judex in causa sua* (or *nemo iudex in sua causa*) another Latin phrase meaning "no-one should be a judge in their own cause." It is a principle of natural justice that no person can judge a case in which they have an interest. "Justice must not only be done but must be obvious to have been done".

If for any reason, these principles are not adhered to, it is for the appellate Court to declare that there has not been a fair hearing and such proceedings must EX DEBITO JUSTICIAE be declared null and void which needs to be struck out. This principle clearly approved by the case law had its root in the common law.

However, let us now consider the position of Islamic law, popularly known and called Sharia Law. The Islamic Legal system equally recognises the principles of fair hearing. I believe it is important to point out that, the foundation of Islamic law can correctly be said to be a religious law, so much as the foundation of the common law of England is.

Thus, it is perhaps pertinent to mention that the common law of England derives its origin from the Ecclesiastical law, which in a general sense means the law relating to any matter concerning the Church of England administered and enforced in any Court. It also can mean the law administered by Ecclesiastical Courts. The Ecclesiastical law of England derives its immediate origin largely from the Canon law of Papal Rome and the Civil law of Imperial Rome.

Qur'an says:

> And now have we set thee (O Muhammad (PBUH)) on a clear road of Our Commandment, so follow it, and follow not the whims of those who know not.
>
> - Qur'an 45:18

Basically, the above Qur'an verses established the doctrine of fair hearing in Islamic Law.

3.7.3 Comparison of Islamic Law with Civil Law

One of the institutions developed by classical Islamic jurists that influenced civil law was the *Hawala*, an early informal value transfer system, which is mentioned in texts of Islamic jurisprudence as early as the 8th century.

Hawala itself later influenced the development of the *Aval* in French civil law and the *Avallo* in Italian law.[41] The "European *commenda*" limited partnerships (Islamic *Qirad*) used in civil law as well as the civil law conception of res *judicata* may also have origins in Islamic law.[42]

3.7.4 International Relations: Islamic Law and International Law Perspectives

Islamic law also made "major contributions" to international admiralty law, departing from the previous Roman and Byzantine maritime laws in several ways.[43] These included Muslim sailors being "paid a fixed wage "in advance" with an understanding that they would owe money in the event of desertion or malfeasance, in keeping with Islamic conventions" in which contracts should specify "a known fee for a known duration".

In contrast to Roman and Byzantine sailors who were "stakeholders in a maritime venture, in as much as captain and crew, with few exceptions, were paid proportional divisions of a sea venture's profit, with shares allotted by rank, only after a voyage's successful conclusion.[44]"

Muslim jurists also distinguished between "coastal navigation, or *cabotage*," and voyages on the "high seas", and they also made shippers "liable for freight in most cases except the seizure of both a ship and its cargo."

Islamic law also "departed from Justinian's *Digest* and the *Nomos Rhodion Nautikos* in condemning slave jettison", and the Islamic *Qirad* was also a precursor to the European *commenda* limited partnership. The "Islamic influence on the development of an international Law of the sea" can thus be discerned alongside that of the Roman influence.[45]

---

[41] **Badr1978pp196**.

[42] *Makdisi 1999*.

[43] H. Khalilieh. *Islamic Maritime Law: An Introduction*. Studies in Islamic law and society. Brill, 1998. ISBN: 9789004109551.

[44] Ibid.

[45] H. Khalilieh. *Admiralty and Maritime Laws in the Mediterranean Sea (ca. 800-1050): The Kita⁻ b Akriyat al-Sufun vis-à-vis the Nomos Rhodion Nautikos*. eng. Vol. 64. Leiden and Boston: Brill, 2006. ISBN: 9789004152533.

3.7.5 Socio-Economic Implications of Islamic Law

Islamic Law classically recognizes only natural persons, and never developed the concept of a legal person, i.e. a legal entity that limits the liabilities of its managers, shareholders and employees which exist beyond the lifetimes of its founders and can own assets, sign contracts and appear in court through representatives.[46]

Thus, Islamic Law has no native tradition of corporate law. This, combined with egalitarian rules of inheritance for male descendants (compared with primogeniture), hindered the concentration of wealth and the development of larger and more sophisticated enterprises, according to Timur Kuran of Duke University. Prohibitions on interest, or "riba" also distinct Muslims from non-Muslim minorities in accessing banks and insurance when these services were first introduced by Westerners. Such factors, according to Qur'an, have played a significant role in retarding economic development in the middle economic crises at the outset of the 21st century when many of the aforementioned economic policies backfired on a global scale and threatened to bankrupt entire countries.[47]

3.7.6 Legal Education in Islam to What Extent?

Fundamentally, the origins of the Ijazah dates back to the *ijazat attadris wa 'l-ifttd* ("license to teach and issue legal opinions") in the medieval Islamic legal education system, which was equivalent to the Doctor of Laws qualification and was developed during the 9th century after the formation of the *Madh'hab* legal schools.

---

[46] T. Kuran. "The Absence of the Corporation in Islamic Law: Origins and Persistence". In: *University of Southern California Center for Law & Social Science (CLASS) Research Paper Series* (2005). URL: https://api.semanticscholar.org/CorpusID:2890366.

[47] T. Kuran. "The logic of financial westernization in the Middle East". In: *Journal of Economic Behavior & Organization* 56.4 (2005). Festschrift in honor of Richard H. Day, pp. 593–615. ISSN: 0167-2681. DOI: https://doi.org/10.1016/j.jebo.2004.04.002. URL: https://www.sciencedirect.com/science/ article/pii/S0167268104001702.

To obtain a doctorate, a student "had to study in a guild school of law, usually four years for the basic undergraduate course" and ten or more years for a post-graduate course. The "doctorate was obtained after an oral examination to determine the originality of the Candidate's theses," and to test the student's "ability to defend them against all objections, in disputations set up for the purpose," which were scholarly exercises practiced throughout the student's "career as a graduate student of law."

After students completed their post-graduate education, they were awarded doctorates giving them the status of *faqih* (meaning "master of law"), *mufti* (meaning "professor of legal opinions") and *mudarris* (meaning "teacher"), which were later translated into Latin as *magister, professor* and *doctor* respectively.[48]

3.7.7 Islamic Law: A Legal System or Legal Tradition?

Islamic law is a legal system, just like the Korean or Indonesian legal system, but not a legal tradition, like the common or civil law tradition. A legal tradition is a set of related beliefs, attitudes, and practices regarding the necessary components of a legal system, including the scope and purposes of the law, the manner in which law is created or discovered, the identity and function of legal actors, and the manner in which law is learned, implemented, developed and adapted.

Basically, the fundamental premises of Islamic law are that God has revealed His will for mankind in the Qur'an and the inspired example of the Prophet Muhammad (PBUH) (SAW), and that society's law must conform to God's revealed guidance. The belief in the Qur'an as God's word and that law should be based on God's command, gives unity to the Islamic legal system.

---

[48] G. Makdisi. "Scholasticism and Humanism in Classical Islam and the Christian West". In: *Journal of the American Oriental Society* 109.2 (1989), pp. 175–182. ISSN: 00030279. URL: http://www.jstor.org/stable/ 604423 (visited on 07/13/2024).

Despite the fact that within Islamic law, there is considerable diversity of opinion over the interpretation of God's revelation and the role of human reason, custom, and other factors in the development of specific rules and regulations yet the system is unique as it strives to fulfil the original aims and objectives that were promulgated by the divine scripture.

4. Introduction to LGBTQ+

Most individuals experience sexual attraction towards those of the opposite gender, which is termed heterosexuality. Nonetheless, a notable minority (estimated at 3–10% in various assessments) consists of men and women exclusively attracted to individuals of the same gender, identifying as homosexual. Between these two ends of the spectrum, there exist intermediary forms of attraction. As early as 1948, sexual orientation has been categorized into seven distinct classifications, spanning from being entirely heterosexual to completely homosexual. For instance, the term "lesbian" denotes a group of women who experience sexual or romantic attraction towards other women. Conversely, "gay" is used to describe men who harbour a sexual or romantic interest in other men. Additionally, "bisexual" pertains to individuals who feel attracted, either sexually or romantically, to both men and women. Moreover, the concept of "transgender" refers to a person whose gender identity or expression defies traditional norms, contrasting with their biologically assigned sex characteristics.[1]

---

[1]   M. I. bin Md Yusof et al. *'Hadith Sahih On Behaviour Of LGBT (Lesbian, Gay, Biseksual And Transgender)'*. Booklet: Accessed July 9, 2023. Department of Islamic Development Malaysia (JAKIM), 2015. URL: https://www.islam.gov.my/images/ePenerbitan/Hadis-hadis_Sahih_Berkaitan_Perlakuan_LGBT_BI.pdf.

Among behavioural traits, sexual orientation (whether heterosexual or homosexual) exhibits one of the most substantial levels of sexual differentiation. This is evident as 90–97% of individuals from one gender experience an attraction distinct from that observed in the opposite gender. Influenced by a range of theories, spanning from Freudian psychoanalysis to social constructivism, sexual orientation has historically and often continued to be perceived as a product of early childhood social experiences. Specifically, theories have suggested that interactions with parents, such as having a dominant or possessive mother, or a distant or absent father, play a role. According to this viewpoint, a new-born baby starts with a neutral sexual orientation "blank slate" (tabula rasa), which then develops based solely on postnatal social interactions. This development could lead in either direction, devoid of any predetermined inclination.[2]

For decades, individuals identifying as homosexuals have faced a multitude of discriminatory practices. These encompass prejudices originating from mental health and medical experts, significantly affecting the well-being of the homosexual community. Professionals within these fields have characterized homosexuals as being outside the norm, pathologically deviating from the standard. In the 1950s, this discriminatory stance was formally endorsed by the American Psychiatric Association (APA) when it categorized homosexuality as a mental disorder. Consequently, the campaign to challenge and overturn the APA's classification became a central objective of the gay rights movement. This pursuit ultimately led to significant milestones, including the official recognition and legalization of same-sex marriage in certain nations.[3]

Advocates of same-sex marriage, including presidents, judges, and prominent figures in the news and entertainment industry, often draw

---

[2]   J. Balthazart. "Minireview: Hormones and human sexual orientation." In: *Endocrinology* 152 8 (2011), pp. 2937– 2947. URL: https://www.ncbi.nlm.nih.gov/pmc/articles/PMC3138231/.

[3]   S. Baughey-Gill. "When Gay Was Not Okay with the APA: A Historical Overview of Homosexuality and its Status as Mental Disorder". In: 2011. URL: https://cedar.wwu.edu/orwwu/vol1/iss1/2.

parallels between their cause and historical milestones like the liberation of slaves following the Civil War or women's suffrage. Their contention is that those who oppose same-sex marriage today parallel those who supported slavery in the past or resisted women's voting rights. Their argument is cunningly clever because it's accurate to point out that denying marriage rights to gay couples constitutes discrimination. For instance, they contend that if a man and a woman can marry, it is discriminatory to deny the same right to a man and a man or a woman and a woman, especially when they are consenting adults in a loving relationship. Thus, their argument revolves around the principles of civil and human rights. However, civil, or human rights protection is typically extended to individuals based on their inherent nature or events that have shaped their circumstances. In simpler terms, it pertains to situations or statuses that are beyond an individual's control- factors that they do not have a say in. Legal safeguards are in place to prevent abuse or discrimination against people due to factors such as gender, race, or disability. These are traits that individuals are born with or events that happen to them, rather than choices they consciously make.[4]

In order to attain the status of a marginalized minority, individuals must demonstrate that their situation is attributed to factors such as genetics (gender, race, disability, etc.), Events (loss of ability, accidents, injuries, etc.), and Circumstances (being both black and impoverished, an immigrant, an ex-convict, etc.). However, Homosexuals do not meet the criteria in any of these categories. For instance, scientific research has indicated that homosexuality is not primarily influenced by genetics. Additionally, no external coercion leads to an individual becoming gay; it is a gradually developing condition often shaped by experiences, environment, and personal choices. Furthermore, homosexuals do not fit the profile of a disadvantaged minority necessitating protective measures.

---

[4]   M. Mazzalongo. *The Wrong Side of History: Gay Marriage*. Review. Accessed July 9, 2023. BibleTalk.tv, 2015. URL: https://bibletalk.tv/the-wrong-side-of-history.

They have wielded substantial influence and hold a prominent position, surpassing other groups in terms of impact and authority.[5]

4.1 Same-Sex Marriage Legalization

They have remarkably managed to promote this notion to the general populace, even in the absence of any substantial corroborating evidence.[6] As a result, they have achieved a substantial legal triumph by effectively employing a facade to establish same-sex marriage as a legal institution across all 50 states of the United States.[7] Furthermore, more than thirty nations have legalized same-sex marriage, while others have granted recognition to same-sex civil unions. However, it's worth noting that the legality of same-sex marriage remains prohibited in numerous countries, and the global advancement of broader LGBTQ+ rights has shown disparities. International entities, including the United Nations, have issued resolutions advocating for LGBTQ+ rights.[8]

4.1.1 United States

Back in 2015, a pivotal decision was made by the U.S. Supreme Court in *Obergefell v. Hodges*, affirming that the Constitution guarantees the right for same-sex couples to enter marriage.[9] The outcome, determined by a 5-4 vote, effectively legalized same-sex marriage across the thirteen states

---

5   Ibid.
6   P. Fagan. *Gay Gene or Broken Family?* Tech. rep. Accessed July 15, 2023. The Catholic Thing, 2010. URL: https://www.thecatholicthing.org/2010/05/27/gay-gene-or-broken-family/.
7   Mazzalongo, *The Wrong Side of History: Gay Marriage.*
8   *Marriage Equality: Global Comparisons.* Backgrounder, News. Accessed July 8, 2023. The Council on Foreign Relations (CFR), 2022. URL: https://www.cfr.org/backgrounder/marriage-equality-global-comparisons.
9   B. Chappell. *Supreme Court Declares Same-Sex Marriage Legal In All 50 States.* America, News. Accessed July 5, 2023. NPR, 2015. URL: https://www.npr.org/sections/thetwo-way/2015/06/26/417717613/supreme-court-rules-all-states-must-allow-same-sex-marriages.

where it had previously been prohibited, and this legalization was also extended to encompass U.S. territories. Recognizing potential concerns that the Supreme Court might allow states to reject the legitimacy of same-sex marriages, Congress acted in 2022. This led to the passing of *the Respect for Marriage Act*, which President Joe Biden signed into law, thereby acknowledging these marriages on a federal level.[10]

4.1.2 Europe

The European Union does not mandate its member states to formally acknowledge same-sex marriage; however, a ruling by the EU's highest court in 2018 stipulates that these nations must ensure the preservation of the rights of same-sex couples to freedom of movement and residence. A significant majority of the countries that have embraced marriage equality are in Western Europe.

The Netherlands (2001), Belgium (2003), Spain (2005), Norway (2009), Sweden (2009), Portugal (2010), Iceland (2010), Denmark (2012), France (2013), the United Kingdom (2013), Luxembourg (2015), Ireland (2015), Finland (2017), Malta (2017), Germany (2017), Austria (2019), and Switzerland (2021) are among the countries where same-sex marriage has been legalized. In Italy, although the parliament endorsed civil unions for same-sex couples in 2016, the legal recognition of same-sex marriage is absent.

Andorra's lawmakers voted in 2022 to transform all existing same-sex civil unions into civil marriages and legalize same-sex marriage. These changes are set to come into effect in early 2023. Simultaneously, Slovenia achieved a significant milestone in 2022 by becoming the first country from the former Yugoslavia to legalize both marriage and adoption for same-sex couples.[11]

---

[10] *Marriage Equality: Global Comparisons.*

[11] Ibid.

4.1.3 **Others**

Canada emerged as a trailblazer in 2005 by becoming the inaugural country within the Western Hemisphere to legalize same-sex marriage. This milestone was subsequently followed by Argentina in 2010, and then Brazil and Uruguay in 2013. Mexico achieved this legal recognition in 2015, followed by Colombia in 2016, Ecuador in 2019, Costa Rica in 2020, and Chile in 2021.

In the realm of sub-Saharan Africa, South Africa stands alone as the sole country where same-sex couples can enter marriage, with the parliament enacting this legalization in 2006. When it comes to the Pacific Rim region, Australia and New Zealand stand as the exclusive nations where same-sex marriage enjoys legal status. In Taiwan, the year 2019 marked a significant turning point as same-sex marriage was formally legalized, aligning with a court ruling issued two years earlier, an action carried out by the legislature.[12]

4.2 **Oppositions**

Amid a steady progression in the acknowledgment of LGBTQ+ rights, an increasing number of nations are moving towards the legalization of same-sex marriage. Nevertheless, opposition to this change remains potent in several other countries. Despite these evolving attitudes, the scope of same-sex marriage legalization remains constricted across a significant portion of Central and Eastern Europe.

To exemplify, in Lithuania, the endorsement for legalizing same-sex marriage stands at 28 percent, while in Ukraine, it is at a mere 14 percent. Meanwhile, Poland and Hungary have witnessed a growth in support in recent times, reaching 47 percent and 49 percent respectively. Despite these increases, both nations uphold the prohibition of same-sex marriage. In Central and Eastern Europe, no less than ten other countries maintain comparable

---

[12]   Ibid.

restrictions. Estonia permits civil unions, although the level of public backing for marriage equality within the Baltic states is notably limited.[13]

Back in 2013, Russia enacted a law that criminalized the dissemination of "propaganda promoting nontraditional sexual relationships among minors." Numerous individuals have faced fines for breaches of this law, which includes engaging in protests and sharing related content on social media platforms. Furthermore, in 2022, Russian President Vladimir Putin endorsed an extension of this ban, broadening its scope. This expansion not only extended the prohibition to the distribution of such materials among adults but also made it unlawful to depict same-sex relationships as "normal." The legal amendments also led to heightened penalties for individuals found in violation of these regulations.[14]

Constitutional bans on same-sex marriage have been established by the governments of Bolivia, Honduras, Nicaragua, and Paraguay. In the year 2022, a court situated in Seoul, South Korea, issued a ruling that withheld recognition of same-sex partnerships, subsequently denying a same-sex couple access to spousal health insurance. This occurred despite prevailing public sentiment in favor of anti-discrimination laws. Within certain regions of Indonesia, Malaysia, and Myanmar, same-sex relationships involving men are prohibited.

Since 2016, Indonesia has witnessed a surge in threats and violence targeting the LGBTQ+ community, a situation highlighted by various human rights organizations. Disturbingly, discriminatory remarks have been made by several public officials. In 2022, Singaporean Prime Minister Lee Hsien Loong pledged to decriminalize gay sex, though he underscored that this change in legislation would not affect the prevailing stance on marriage.[15]

In Brunei, engaging in gay sexual activity is met with the severe punishment of death by stoning, although the government, in response

---

[13]   Ibid.
[14]   Ibid.
[15]   *Marriage Equality: Global Comparisons.*

to the global outcry, has declared its intention not to carry out this law. Moreover, numerous countries in South and Central Asia, such as Bangladesh and Pakistan, have criminalized same-sex relationships. Afghanistan has consistently exhibited low levels of support for same-sex marriage.

Furthermore, across a considerable part of the Middle East and North Africa, same-sex relations remain unlawful, and nations such as Iran, Saudi Arabia, and Yemen enforce the death penalty for such actions. Algeria, Morocco, Oman, Syria, Tunisia, and Gaza have specific legislation in place that explicitly outlaws same-sex acts. In numerous parts of the African continent, same-sex relations are against the law and are subject to capital punishment in Mauritania and Sudan, as well as in certain areas of Nigeria and Somalia.[16]

As previously discussed, the United States was not the pioneer in legalizing same-sex marriage. Nevertheless, the U.S. strongly asserts itself as a global authority, and the official recognition of same-sex marriage is a clear indication of this posture. This development has given rise to a shift where what was once deemed unusual has now become the norm, causing a gradual erosion of the concept of sanity.

The rationale behind the haste to establish legal support for same-sex marriage raises questions. Despite scientific consensus in various medical disciplines indicating that the causes of same-sex attraction are not health-related, innate, biological, or linked to prenatal factors, countries have pressed forward with this legalization. The prohibition of any endeavors by psychologists, who believed that orientation could be altered through practices referred to as "conversion therapy," remains puzzling to many.

Even if the hypothesis of inborn causes for same-sex attraction were accurate, should not those who aspire to change their orientation be permitted to do so? Additionally, should not experts who hold the belief that such orientations can be altered be afforded the benefit of consideration?

---

[16] Ibid.

The potential negative consequences associated with the legalization of same-sex marriage across Europe and the Western world prompted Barbara Blewstar, a former member of the Arizona State of Representatives, to assert that "the perversion that follows homosexuality is bestiality and then human sacrifice and cannibalism".[17] Undoubtedly, the legalization of same-sex marriage has the capacity to trigger demands for additional contentious rights, which, given time, may eventually be granted. This trajectory could lead to an ongoing cycle, ultimately blurring the distinction between what is ethically right and legally sanctioned. A disheartening aspect of our current era is the shifting perception, where individuals who uphold moral correctness are sometimes labeled as aberrant due to their divergence from what is merely legally defined as right.

4.3 Early Views of Homosexuality

In the early stages, perceptions of homosexuality in the Western world were deeply influenced by religious principles. A widely held perspective within religious contexts posited that sexual activity was designated solely for the purpose of procreation. Consequently, homosexual actions were deemed sinful due to their inability to lead to reproduction. These religious outlooks also influenced the shaping of secular legal systems.

As the 16th century unfolded, England began to regard homosexuality as a serious offense, even punishable by death. This marked a significant turn in the criminalization of same-sex relationships. The United States also followed suit, introducing laws criminalizing homosexual conduct, thereby perpetuating these perspectives well into the 20th century.[18]

---

[17] L. J. Taylor. *Gay Marriage*. mirrored in the philosophy section: Accessed July 8, 2023. Jonelin, 1999. URL: https://jonelin.tripod.com/politics/gay.htm.

[18] Baughey-Gill, "When Gay Was Not Okay with the APA: A Historical Overview of Homosexuality and its Status as Mental Disorder"; K. S. Morgan and R. M. Nerison. "Homosexuality and psychopolitics: An historical overview." In: *Psychotherapy* 30 (1993), pp. 133–140. DOI: https://doi.org/10.1037/0033-3204.30.1.133. URL: https://psycnet.apa.org/record/1994-25249-001.

Furthermore, a comparable perspective on homosexuality persisted within the medical community of the 19th century. During this period, homosexuality was regarded as a moral failing, as individuals were seen as actively choosing to commit a "sin." To counteract this perceived vice, medical experts focused their efforts on identifying and remedying the underlying cause of homosexual behaviour.

Amid this context, neurologist Jean-Martin Charcot, in the 1860s, postulated that homosexuality was inherent rather than acquired from external influences. His viewpoint was based on observations that indicated homosexuality did not respond to hypnotic treatments. However, differing viewpoints emerged among researchers, with one notable example being Richard von Krafft-Ebing, a German psychiatrist recognized for his early studies on sexual deviance. Krafft-Ebing asserted that various sexual deviations, including homosexuality, arose due to a combination of inherited and environmental factors. Consequently, these experts perceived non-procreative sexual behaviours as forms of psychopathology, attributing this perspective to their belief that such behaviours lacked evolutionary adaptiveness.[19]

In contrast to the predominant view among 19th-century researchers, which considered homosexuality as aberrant, a small number of individuals such as Havelock Ellis, a British sexologist, and Dr. Magnus Hirschfeld, a homosexual physician, held the perspective that homosexuality was not a pathological condition but rather a normal variation within human sexuality. However, the stance of this minority, which regarded homosexuality as non-pathological, was further undermined in 1952 with the publication of the first edition of the Diagnostic and Statistical Manual of Mental Disorders (DSM) by the APA. In this inaugural edition, homosexuality was categorized as a "sociopathic personality disturbance." This classification persisted in

---

[19]   Baughey-Gill, "When Gay Was Not Okay with the APA: A Historical Overview of Homosexuality and its Status as Mental Disorder".

the subsequent edition, published in 1968, where homosexuality was reclassified as a sexual deviation.[20]

The categorization of homosexuality as a mental disorder by the APA had significant ramifications, affecting both the homosexual community and the broader perception of homosexuality within society. Given the APA's assertion that this classification was grounded in scientific research, it proved challenging for individuals identifying as homosexuals to contest perspectives that labelled them as deviant. Consequently, the efforts of gay and lesbian individuals to secure recognition as ordinary members of mainstream society faced additional hurdles due to a medical diagnosis that insinuated their deviance and abnormality.

4.4 Removal of homosexuality from the DSM list

During the 1973 APA convention, a consensus was reached that, as per their definition, homosexuality did not meet the criteria for being classified as a mental disorder. Subsequently, on December 15, 1973, the APA's Board of Trustees officially eliminated homosexuality from the DSM. While many members of the APA endorsed this step to remove homosexuality from the DSM, some criticized it as a hastily made political move lacking substantial evidence grounded in thorough research.

To address some of these reservations, the APA organized a vote in 1974 among its members regarding the exclusion of homosexuality from the DSM. Ultimately, 58% of the voters supported the 1973 decision, leading to the continued omission of homosexuality from the DSM as a distinct clinical disorder. Despite ongoing debates, the APA remained steadfast

---

[20] Baughey-Gill, "When Gay Was Not Okay with the APA: A Historical Overview of Homosexuality and its Status as Mental Disorder"; J. Drescher. "Queer Diagnoses Parallels and Contrasts in the History of Homosexuality, Gender Variance, and the Diagnostic and Statistical Manual (DSM) Review and Recommendations Prepared for the DSM-V Sexual and Gender Identity Disorders Work Group". In: *FOCUS* 18.3 (2020), pp. 308–335. DOI: 10.1176 / appi.focus.18302. eprint: https://doi.org /10.1176/ appi.focus.18302. URL: https://doi.org/10.1176/appi.focus.18302.

in its choice and embarked on a gradual process of garnering backing for acknowledging homosexuality as a normative facet.[21]

In a possible attempt to address concerns raised against the 1973 decision, a subsequent revision of the DSM emerged as DSM II in 1974. This new version replaced the term "homosexuality" with "Sexual Orientation Disturbance." This categorization deemed homosexuality an ailment solely if an individual was "disturbed by, in conflict with, or wished to change their sexual orientation." It was emphasized that homosexuality did not qualify as a psychiatric disorder. A subsequent iteration of the manual, the DSM-III, published in 1980, further renamed "Sexual Orientation Disturbance" as "Ego Dystonic Homosexuality." However, this classification was eventually removed in a subsequent revision in 1987.[22] Consequently, while some critics viewed the initial decision to expel homosexuality from the DSM as rushed, it took more than 14 years from the original ruling for homosexuality to be fully eliminated from the manual.[23]

---

[21]   Baughey-Gill, "When Gay Was Not Okay with the APA: A Historical Overview of Homosexuality and its Status as Mental Disorder".

[22]   Drescher, "Queer Diagnoses Parallels and Contrasts in the History of Homosexuality, Gender Variance, and the Diagnostic and Statistical Manual (DSM) Review and Recommendations Prepared for the DSM-V Sexual and Gender Identity Disorders Work Group".

[23]   Baughey-Gill, "When Gay Was Not Okay with the APA: A Historical Overview of Homosexuality and its Status as Mental Disorder".

5. Argument for and Against Homosexuality by Scientist

O nce more, a schism among researchers has rekindled the debate surrounding same-sex marriage. As a result, a divide has emerged in the conclusions drawn about the underlying factors contributing to same-sex attraction. Certain groups, who exhibit an understanding of same-sex attraction, have posited a theory that attributes its origins to prenatal influences, biological factors, and distinctions in a specific brain segment's size between homosexual men and heterosexual females. Conversely, another faction, driven by inclusivity and the absence of substantial substantiation or replication of experiments linking same-sex attraction to prenatal causes and other elements, has refuted the theory advocated by those sympathetic to same-sex attraction.[1]

---

[1]   S. M. Breedlove. "Prenatal Influences on Human Sexual Orientation: Expectations versus Data". In: *Seattle J. Soc. Just.* 46.6 (Feb. 2017), 1583–1592. DOI: 10.1007/s10508-016-0904-2. URL: https://digitalcommons. law.seattleu.edu/sjsj/vol2/iss2/24/; w. h. james. "Biological and psychosocial determinants of male and female human sexual orientation". In: *Journal of Biosocial Science* 37.5 (2005), 555–567. DOI: 10.1017/S0021932004007059.

5.1 **The Brain Theory**

Simon LeVay, a neuroscientist affiliated with the esteemed Salk Institute for Biological Studies situated in La Jolla, California, United States, postulated that the brain's structure might potentially underlie the sexual inclinations and conduct of individuals identifying as homosexuals. LeVay's hypothesis hinged on the notion that if the brains of homosexual men were shown to resemble those of heterosexual women more closely than those of heterosexual men, brain structure could influence their sexual preferences. Subsequently, he conducted a study involving the examination of 41 cadavers' brains.

His research yielded the observation that a specific region known as the interstitial nuclei of the anterior hypothalamus 3 (INAH3) was comparably smaller in homosexual men in comparison to heterosexual men, and additionally, this region was also smaller in women when compared to heterosexual men. LeVay extrapolated from these findings that they signify the potential to explore the facet of human nature- sexual orientation- at a biological level using biological tools, rather than solely relying on psychiatric approaches.[2]

The media elevated the publication to a sensational level, leading the public to adopt the perception that the neuroscientist had conclusively unraveled the enigma behind why certain individuals identify as gay while the majority identify as straight. Despite robust criticism of LeVay's study from various academic domains, the media's portrayal managed to firmly establish the notion that homosexuality represented a natural and biologically determined variation from heterosexuality. LeVay's study emerged during a period when the active struggle for gay and lesbian rights was highly prominent in both the United States and Canada. In their article titled "Scientific Communications

---

[2]   T. H. M. II and N. Zamichow. *Study Ties Part of Brain to Men's Sexual Orientation : Medicine: San Diego researcher's findings offer first evidence of a biological cause for homosexuality.* Science & Medicine. Los Angeles Times, 1991; S. LeVay. "A Difference in Hypothalamic Structure Between Heterosexual and Homosexual Men". In: *Science* 253.5023 (1991), pp. 1034–1037. DOI: 10 . 1126 / science . 1887219. eprint: https://www.science.org/doi/pdf/10.1126/science.1887219. URL: https://www.science.org/doi/abs/10.1126/science.1887219.

about Biological Influences on Homosexuality and the Politics of Gay Rights," Garretson and Sunhay delve into the political climate that fostered the requirement for a scientific rationale for homosexuality. Furthermore, as a self-identified gay individual, LeVay's motivations were inherently political in his quest to identify the biological determinants of homosexuality.

In this pursuit, LeVay aimed to contribute to the ongoing political discourse surrounding the equality of gay and lesbian individuals. His objective was to provide evidence that homosexuality is innate (not a conscious choice) and that homosexuals deserve the same civil rights and liberties as their heterosexual counterparts. The substantial popularity his article garnered sheds light on how the public perceives sexual orientation and demonstrates how societal and political structures shape scientific interpretations of human biology.[3]

In response to LeVay's theory, scientists have critiqued his proposition and raised significant concerns that undermined its validity. Notably, Byne and Parson challenged the theory by highlighting that LeVay's findings rested on assumptions rather than established facts. They further emphasized that the involvement of INAH3 in the development of sexual orientation remains undetermined. Moreover, a noteworthy factor is that Dr. Simon LeVay lacked knowledge about the sexual histories of the cadavers he examined.

Complicating matters, a substantial proportion of his subjects had succumbed to AIDS, a condition caused by HIV. This suggests that the brain, including the Hypothalamus which plays a pivotal role in the immune system, might have been impacted in various ways. Consequently, the distinctions in INAH3 size that LeVay linked to sexual orientation could conceivably be attributed to fluctuations in testosterone levels arising from AIDS or its treatment.[4]

---

[3]   M. McLaughlin. "Is There a Gay Brain? The Problems with Scientific Research of Sexual Orientation". In: *The Great Lakes Journal of Undergraduate History* 6.1 (2018), pp. 45–59. URL: https://scholar.uwindsor.ca/gljuh/vol6/iss1/4.

[4]   W. Byne. "Interview: The Biological Evidence for Homosexuality Reappraised". In: *Issues in Religion and Psychotherapy* 19.1 (1993), pp. 17–27. URL: https://scholarsarchive.byu.edu/irp/vol19/iss1/3.

Dr. Byne pointed out a significant limitation in LeVay's study, noting that LeVay handled all aspects of the research process independently-from collecting the brains to conducting measurements and performing statistical analysis. Within this realm of research, the conventional practice mandates that measurements be conducted by multiple investigators before presenting a study with such provocative and politically sensitive implications.[5]

Subsequently, Dr. LeVay acknowledged that his assertion of a link between this brain structure and sexual orientation could not establish causation or even determine the direction of influence. He further conceded that the findings did not provide the means to ascertain whether the size of INAH3 in an individual served as the cause or the consequence of that individual's sexual orientation.[6]

5.2 Anterior Commissure Theory

To establish a correlation between brain size and homosexuality, L. S. Allen and R. A. Gorski reported in 1991 that a brain region known as the 'Anterior Commissure' exhibited larger dimensions in homosexuals compared to heterosexual men.[7] However, this theory faced immediate criticism through the research conducted by Mitchell S. Lasco and colleagues. Their investigation involved analyzing the cross-sectional area of the anterior commissure in postmortem samples from 120 individuals. Their findings indicated no discernible differences in the

---

[5] Ibid.

[6] *Researcher Simon LeVay Talks About the Science of Sexuality*. News. Accessed July 11, 2023. the Office of Marketing and Communications, Elmhurst University, 2012. URL: https://www.elmhurst.edu/news/researcher-simon-levay-talks-about-the-science-of-sexuality/.

[7] L. S. Allen and R. A. Gorski. "Sexual orientation and the size of the anterior commissure in the human brai." In: *Proceedings of the National Academy of Sciences of the United States of America* 89 15 (1992), pp. 7199–202. DOI: https://doi.org/10.1073/pnas.89.15.7199. URL: https://pubmed.ncbi.nlm.nih.gov/1496013/.

anterior commissure's size concerning factors like age, HIV status, gender, or sexual orientation.[8]

To reinforce the perspective presented by Mitchell S. Lasco's study, Byne and Parsons further elaborated that even if Allen and Gorski's findings were replicable, the magnitude of overlap in anterior commissure size between homosexual and heterosexual men rendered it ineffective as a determinant of an individual's sexual orientation.[9]

5.3 The Twin Theory

J. Michael Bailey and Richard C. Palliard proposed a theory that posited a greater incidence of homosexuality among identical (monozygotic) and fraternal (dizygotic) twins compared to adoptive siblings. Their findings firmly indicated that among relatives identified as homosexual, 52% were monozygotic co-twins, 22% were dizygotic co-twins, 9% were non-twin biological brothers, and 11% of adoptive brothers exhibited homosexuality.[10]

Once more, Byne and Parson, along with Dr. Neil Whitehead, raised objections to this theory. Dr. Byne pointed out that studies of this nature lack the ability to effectively differentiate between biological and environmental influences because genetically related individuals also share environmental factors. Dr. Byne used the analogy of Protestantism running in families, illustrating that shared family traits are not necessarily genetic in nature.[11]

In response, a series of eight significant studies were conducted over the course of more than two decades, involving over 10,000 pairs of identical twins. These studies collectively reached a consistent conclusion: that the

[8] M. S. Lasco et al. "A lack of dimorphism of sex or sexual orientation in the human anterior commissure". In: *Brain Research* 936.1 (2002), pp. 95–98. ISSN: 0006-8993. DOI: https://doi.org/10.1016/S0006-8993(02)02590- URL: https://www.sciencedirect.com/science/article/pii/S0006899302025908.

[9] L. D. Wardle. "The Biological Causes and Consequences of Homosexual Behavior and Their Relevance for Family Law and Policies". In: *DePaul Law Review* 56.997 (2006), pp. 997 –1034. DOI: https://doi.org/10. 1073/pnas.89.15.7199. URL: https://ssrn.com/abstract=2329817.

[10] Ibid.

[11] Byne, "Interview: The Biological Evidence for Homosexuality Reappraised".

concept of individuals being born homosexual was not substantiated. This line of research led Dr. Neil Whitehead, a PhD holder in biochemistry and statistics, to deduce that the lack of a discernible link between homosexuality and the twin theory indicated that genetics played a minor role in the origins of homosexuality.

Identical twins possess identical genes or DNA and are raised in equivalent parental environments. Consequently, if homosexuality were determined solely by genetics or parental conditions, one would expect that if one twin is gay, the co-twin would inevitably also be gay. However, when both twins are not gay, it challenges the notion of homosexuality being genetically pre-determined. Byne and Parsons further argued that if homosexuality were entirely governed by a person's genetic makeup, it would be anticipated that 100% of identical monozygotic twins of homosexuals would also be homosexual. However, this is not observed in practice. In fact, the intriguing aspect of these twin studies is the significant proportion of monozygotic twins who differ in their sexual orientation despite sharing both their genetic makeup and prenatal and family environments.[12] This collection of evidence suggests that the primary factors contributing to homosexuality in one identical twin while not affecting the other must be post-birth influences.

To sum up, Dr. Byne highlighted that the prevailing inclination towards biological interpretations of sexual orientation arises largely due to discontent with the current state of psychosocial explanations, rather than being driven by the inherent potency of biological evidence itself. Upon critically assessing recent genetic, hormonal, and neuroanatomical evidence concerning sexual orientation, we find that it falls short of being convincing, as indicated in our review.[13]

---

[12] *Identical Twins Studies Prove Homosexuality is Not Genetic.* Featured. Accessed July 13, 2023. The Aquila Report, 2013. URL: https://theaquilareport.com/identical-twins-studies-prove-homosexuality-is-not-genetic/; Wardle, "The Biological Causes and Consequences of Homosexual Behavior and Their Relevance for Family Law and Policies".

[13] Byne, "Interview: The Biological Evidence for Homosexuality Reappraised".

5.4 Hormonal Deficiency Theory

Based on studies conducted on rats, certain scientists put forth a hypothesis suggesting that human males exposed to notably below-average levels of prenatal testosterone and human females exposed to significantly above-average levels of prenatal testosterone might have a heightened likelihood of developing a homosexual orientation in their adult lives.[14] Once more, this theory has faced scrutiny from scientists due to the approach taken in comparing hormonal levels in rats with those in humans. Byne and Parsons elaborate on this, highlighting the complexities inherent in extrapolating from mating behaviors and postures observed in rodents to the intricate psychological processes in humans. They emphasize that motivated sexual behaviors in humans are unlikely to be governed by the rigid endocrine control seen in rodents. As such, the suitability of rodent behavior as a model for understanding motivated sexual behavior in humans remains questionable. The intricate range and adaptability of human sexual behaviors cannot easily be reduced to factors as straightforward as how a female rat reacts to a male.[15]

5.5 Conclusion from the Health-Based Theories of Causes of Homosexuality

Evidently, based on the considerations, there is no definitive underlying cause of same-sex attraction from a perspective rooted in health abnormalities. All theories emerging from this viewpoint that lean towards supporting the case for same-sex marriage are either riddled with methodological flaws, intentionally manipulated to validate same-sex attraction, or constructed through selective sampling of subjects for observations or experiments in support of the same. Even The American Gay and Lesbian Medical

---

[14]   Balthazart, "Minireview: Hormones and human sexual orientation."
[15]   Wardle, "The Biological Causes and Consequences of Homosexual Behavior and Their Relevance for Family Law and Policies"; Byne, "Interview: The Biological Evidence for Homosexuality Reappraised".

Association cautioned against using the argument that homosexuality is biologically determined due to insufficient evidence. The theories positioning same-sex attraction as an ailment beyond the control of those affected by prenatal or biological factors lack credibility due to the absence of subsequent research to validate, reproduce, or substantiate such propositions.

6. Psychologist View of Causes of Homosexuality

F reud, a renowned psychoanalyst, held the belief that inherent bisexuality is a natural aspect of all humans, and he posited that exclusive homosexuality indicates a halt in typical sexual development. Furthermore, he did not consider homosexuality to be treatable or even require treatment. In his capacity as a clinician, he declined to offer therapy to homosexuals unless the treatment was targeting an issue unrelated to the patient's sexual orientation. However, it's important to note that many other psychoanalysts did not align with Freud's viewpoints on this matter.[1]

Shortly after Freud's passing, most psychoanalysts publicly distanced themselves from his viewpoints. These post-Freudian psychoanalysts regarded homosexuality as an attempt by individuals to find sexual satisfaction when conventional heterosexual options seemed too intimidating. According to them, homosexuality was perceived as a manifestation of an underlying disorder necessitating therapeutic intervention.[2] For instance, a prominent psychoanalyst named Irving Bieber, active during the 1950s and 60s, believed that homosexuality

---

[1]   Baughey-Gill, "When Gay Was Not Okay with the APA: A Historical Overview of Homosexuality and its Status as Mental Disorder".

[2]   Morgan and Nerison, "Homosexuality and psychopolitics: An historical overview."; K. Lewes. *The Psychoanalytic Theory of Male Homosexuality*. Wilensky-Ritzenhein Gay Book Collection. Simon and Schuster, 1988. ISBN: 9780671623913.

was a consequence of problematic parent-child relationships. Focusing exclusively on gay men, he asserted that their sexual orientation resulted from over-involved, enticing mothers, and aloof, hostile fathers.[3] Additionally, he advocated for early intervention to identify and address signs of what he called "pre-homosexual" boys to prevent the development of homosexuality.[4]

Besides psychoanalysis, numerous approaches for treating homosexuality were endorsed during the 19th and early 20th centuries. Records indicate the utilization of electroshock therapy, hypnosis, lobotomy, and assorted behavioral methods including abstinence and aversion therapy, all aimed at addressing and "curing" homosexuality.[5] Broadly, psychoanalysts persisted as one of the final groups within the medical community to publicly regard homosexuality as a treatable mental disorder. This perspective endured even after the classification was removed from the DSM in 1973.[6]

6.1 Post-birth and Environmental Factors

It is widely acknowledged that a deficiency of love from a same-sex parent, leading to an emotional void, often drives many individuals towards homosexuality to compensate for this absence. Dr. William Consiglio, an experienced researcher in the field of homosexuality's causes and treatment, characterized homosexuality as a deviation from the mainstream path of heterosexual development. He posited that homosexuality is not an inherent trait but rather a result of sexual disorientation when the natural course of heterosexuality is obstructed. Consiglio emphasized that homosexuality is

---

[3] Balthazart, "Minireview: Hormones and human sexual orientation."
[4] Baughey-Gill, "When Gay Was Not Okay with the APA: A Historical Overview of Homosexuality and its Status as Mental Disorder".
[5] Morgan and Nerison, "Homosexuality and psychopolitics: An historical overview."; J. Drescher and J. Merlino. *American Psychiatry and Homosexuality: An Oral History*. Taylor & Francis, 2012. ISBN: 9781136859939.
[6] Baughey-Gill, "When Gay Was Not Okay with the APA: A Historical Overview of Homosexuality and its Status as Mental Disorder".

not an alternative sexual orientation but rather an emotional disorientation stemming from an interrupted or blocked emotional development within the heterosexual context.

It is crucial to recognize that numerous factors, both abstract and concrete, influence a child's sexual orientation. Dr. William Consiglio coined the term "conspiracy of factors" to describe the myriad psychological elements that converge, often at the right time and in the right proportions, to steer a developing child's sexual desires. Sigmund Freud, an Austrian psychiatrist and the originator of psychoanalytic psychology, proposed that a homosexual male child is shaped by a dominant mother and a passive, indifferent, or antagonistic father, and vice versa. This theory underscores the role of parenting in a child's life and emphasizes the shared responsibility of both parents in providing a comprehensive emotional education for the child.

Furthermore, this notion also implies the significant repercussions a child might face when one aspect of parenting is absent- either due to a lack of presence, indifference, or a lack of commitment from a father or an excessively distant mother. A child relies on guidance and active involvement from both parents to ensure a well-rounded and comprehensive emotional upbringing. Achieving emotional equilibrium holds paramount importance in a child's psychological development, contributing not only to their interpersonal relationships but also enhancing their cognitive growth.

Both parents need to collaborate effectively to provide the child with a solid emotional foundation. This entails finding a harmonious balance between the nurturing qualities of the mother and the assertive attributes of the father to foster a psychologically stable environment for the child's emotional maturity. Recent data underscores the essential role of both parents in a child's emotional growth. Notably, the lowest rate of lesbian behavior, at 4%, was observed among women raised in intact married families. In comparison, the rates increased to 6% and 6.6% for those raised in married stepfamilies, divorced single-parent or always single-parent households. The highest rate, reaching 9.6%, was observed among those who were brought up in households where the girl's mother cohabited with a man who was not her father.[7]

In her book titled "Homosexuality: A New Christian Ethic," Dr. Elizabeth Moberly not only aligned with the perspectives of various psychologists regarding the origins of homosexuality but also highlighted the multifaceted nature of homosexual conditions that often elude common understanding. Within this complexity, there exists a consistent factor: an inadequacy in the relationship with the parent of the same sex, driving an urge to compensate for this deficit through same-sex relationships. It's worth noting that this deficit might not necessarily be intentional on the parent's part; nonetheless, it can disrupt the necessary attachment crucial for healthy psychological and sexual development during a pivotal phase in the child's life.[8]

Dr. Joseph Nicolosi, a clinical psychologist specializing in reparative therapy, concurs with other psychologists regarding the potential factors contributing to homosexuality. He identifies additional influences such as "a hostile older brother who is feared, a mother with a warm and captivating personality who becomes more appealing to the boy than an emotionally distant father, a mother who actively disapproves of masculinity, childhood experiences of being seduced by another male, peer labels linked to athleticism or timidity, contemporary cultural elements that steer a confused and uncertain youth toward the embracing gay community, and within the boy himself, a particularly sensitive and somewhat delicate disposition." Other variables encompass feelings of self-esteem and an inferiority complex that can harm the child's self-perception, unresolved needs for affection, encounters with social or emotional traumas, early engagement in masturbation, exposure to pornography, or premature exploration of sexual experiences during childhood that can generate misunderstanding

---

[7]   Fagan, *Gay Gene or Broken Family?*

[8]   S. A. Cundale. "'HOMOSEXUALITY'. A NEW CHRISTIAN ETHIC By Elizabeth R. Moberly. Published by James Clarke". In: *International Journal of Social Psychiatry* 29.3 (1983), pp. 238–238. DOI: 10 . 1177 / 002076408302900317. eprint: https://doi. org/10.1177/002076408302900317. URL: https://doi.org/10.1177/002076408302900317.

and confusion, thereby reinforcing homosexual inclinations due to the absence of comprehension. Notably, children subjected to sexual abuse or youth who experience early sexual contact can grapple with confusion, leading to gender-misidentified perceptions and unconventional sexual interests and values. Research has demonstrated that boys who undergo sexual abuse are four to seven times more prone to experience same-sex attraction, with 65% of victims indicating that the abuse affected their sexual identity.

6.2 Conclusion from Psychologists' Point of View on the Causes of Homosexuality

From the perspective of psychologists, it is the post-birth or environmental elements that emerge as the significant catalysts or origins of same-sex attraction. Interestingly, this viewpoint aligns with the consensus among most scientists who acknowledge that the diverse contributing factors to same-sex attraction lack robust medical explanations due to insufficient and inconclusive evidence supporting the various prenatal theories. Consequently, they assert that the origins or influences behind same-sex attractions are more closely linked to post-birth or environmental factors. Some experts assert with confidence that being gay is not an innate trait from birth, thereby further solidifying the psychologists' emphasis on environmental factors as the primary force shaping the sexual orientation of homosexuality.

7. Homosexuality from a Religious Standpoint

In this exploration, we will delve into the scriptures of the two Abrahamic faiths (Christianity and Islam) to assess their responses to homosexual conduct. It's important to highlight that these religions do not present any explicit theories or discussions on homosexuality; rather, they unequivocally condemn such behaviour and outline the consequences for those involved in such actions.

7.1 Christian View on Homosexuality

Certain Christians continue to maintain the belief that homosexuality is not only perceived as a mental disorder but is also viewed as a tool utilized by a figure known as Satan, leading to sin and an abomination. This viewpoint is supported by individuals like Barbara Blewster, a member of the Church of Latter-Day Saints, and the Arizona State Legislature. On the other hand, there are Christians who either support homosexual behaviour or identify as homosexual themselves, emphasizing Jesus' commandment to love one another as paramount, transcending minor references to same-sex relationships.

An intriguing aspect of differing moral perspectives within the same religious framework is the interpretation of heterosexual marriage as the cornerstone of Christian life. A representative from the National Clergy Council cautioned that allowing homosexuals to celebrate their unions through state-recognized marriage might trigger a substantial breakdown of "values." Contrarily, those with a more liberal Christian stance contend that Christian morality is not solely founded on marriage, but rather on embodying Christ's principles, as articulated by the Apostle Paul in 1 Corinthians 11:1. It's important to note that Jesus himself did not conform to the norms of an average married Christian. His teachings did not advocate for followers to take on spouses and emulate him. Instead, he urged them to embrace their crosses, as conveyed in Mark 8:34, and even to forsake their families and homes, an act exemplified by his disciples, as referenced in Luke 18:29-30.[1]

These considerations bring us to a pivotal question regarding the legitimacy of same-sex marriage: Should homosexuals be granted the sacred status of matrimony akin to heterosexual couples, or should it be denied on the premise that homosexuality is not perceived as sanctified?

7.1.1 Biblical Perspectives

Throughout history, religion has exerted a significant influence in establishing norms for socially acceptable manifestations of gender and sexuality. Beliefs concerning gender roles and their appropriate delineations between men and women have deep origins in traditions like Judeo-Christian teachings. In these traditions, the defiance of gender norms is often deemed deserving of condemnation, rebuke, and in some instances, even severe penalties including death. Considering the historical entanglement of gender presentation and sexual inclination, the biblical proscriptions against homosexuality occasionally employ phrasing that characterizes men as straying from their innate, divinely ordained gender roles:

---

[1]   Taylor, *Gay Marriage*.

Thou shalt not lie with mankind, as with womankind: it is an abomination.

- Leviticus 18:22

If a man also lies with mankind, as he lieth with a woman, both of them have committed an abomination: they shall surely be put to death; their blood shall be upon them.

- Leviticus 20:13

Just as Sodom and Gomorrah and the surrounding cities, which likewise indulged in sexual immorality and pursued unnatural desire, serve as an example by undergoing a punishment of eternal fire.

- Jude 1:7

And likewise, also the men, leaving the natural use of the woman, burned in their lust one toward another; men with men working that which is unseemly, and receiving in themselves that recompense of their error which was meet.

- Romans 1:27

Know ye not that the unrighteous shall not inherit the kingdom of God? Be not deceived: neither fornicators, nor idolaters, nor adulterers, nor effeminate, nor abusers of themselves with mankind, nor thieves, nor covetous, nor drunkards, nor revilers, nor extortioners, shall inherit the kingdom of God.

- I Corinthians 6:9

The Bible's stance on this matter is unequivocal. The message is straightforward and unambiguous: homosexuality is prohibited, and the mentioned verses explicitly outline the appropriate consequences for those who engage in such acts. Despite this stern admonition, governments in the UK, US, and Europe have managed to influence Christianity and have even orchestrated scenarios where pastors facilitate same-sex weddings within churches.

In addition to addressing sexual violations, certain passages in the Bible touch on what could be referred to today as transvestism and transsexualism. For instance, the Bible explicitly prohibits cross-dressing:

> The clothes of a man shall not be put on a woman, nor shall a man wear woman's garments; for whoever does these things is an abomination to the Lord.
>
> - Deuteronomy 22:5

In addition, within orthodox Jewish practices, Leviticus says:

> And ye shall not offer unto the LORD that which is bruised, or crushed, or broken, or cut; neither shall ye make any offering thereof in your land.
>
> - Leviticus 22:24

This is interpreted to include a prohibition against castrating both animals and humans, which is further extended to forbid procedures such as sex reassignment surgery.

7.1.2 A Debatable Marriage

A significant portion of the ongoing discourse regarding same-sex marriage centers on fundamental disparities in religious viewpoints concerning marriage. While marriage is acknowledged as one of the seven sacraments solely within the Catholic tradition among Christian denominations, all Christian traditions regard marriage as having a sacramental nature. Marriage, along with other sacraments like Holy Orders, reconciliation, and anointing, serves as pivotal "rites of passage" that have been present across various cultures for centuries. In Christian teachings, the term "sacrament" signifies a symbol of God's tangible manifestation among humanity.[2]

Within the public discourse surrounding same-sex marriage, the Christian religious stance has been equally prominent alongside legislative reactions. The Episcopal Church remains divided due to the election and consecration of Reverend Gene Robinson, an openly gay priest, as the Bishop of New Hampshire.[3] Simultaneously, Bishop David Bena of Albany, New York, represented a group of thirty-six dissenting bishops from the United States and Canada, expressing their reservations:

> "It is impossible to affirm a candidate for bishop and symbol of unity whose very consecration is dividing the whole Anglican communion."

Bena highlighted that Bishop Robinson's way of life was inconsistent with scripture and the doctrines of this church.

In the context of the Roman Catholic Church, the Vatican has recently released a document that articulates its stance against granting legal recognition to same-sex unions, specifically marriage. The document titled "Considerations Regarding Proposals to Give Legal Recognition to Unions Between Homosexual Persons" does not present novel arguments but rather reaffirms the Church's longstanding positions against same-sex relationships and the affirmation of marriage as a sacred union between a man and a woman. Furthermore, in September 2003, the U.S. Catholic Bishops' Conference endorsed a federal marriage amendment to the Constitution.[4]

Mike Mazzalongo, a preacher and educator at a ministry in Montreal, Quebec, expressed the viewpoint that American society, influenced by

---

[2]   G. Chamberlain. "A Religious Argument for Same-Sex Marriage". In: *Seattle J. Soc. Just.* 2.2 (Mar. 2004), pp. 494–503. URL: https://digitalcommons.law.seattleu.edu/sjsj/vol2/iss2/24/.

[3]   Ibid.

[4]   Ibid.

years of morally questionable entertainment, influenced by a secular news media and educational system, and influenced by a powerful and well-connected gay advocacy group, has embraced the unsubstantiated idea that two individuals of the same gender should have the right to marry each other, complete with all the privileges that heterosexual couples enjoy. He further emphasized that throughout history, the one fundamental principle universally agreed upon by various cultures and religions is that marriage is the optimal context for raising children. This, he stressed, is the one capability that same-sex couples lack. While they can enter marriage, engage in intimate relationships, establish a home, and share their lives for decades, they are unable to procreate, which is the fundamental, ethical, human, and societal purpose of marriage in its essence.[5]

7.1.3 Consequences of Reversing Moral Order

In the present day, we possess more nuanced methods of dismantling the moral framework established by God in His Scriptures. The Bible has conveyed that:

> Woe to those who call evil good, and good evil; Who substitute darkness for light and light for darkness; Who substitutes bitter for sweet and sweet for bitter!
>
> - Isaiah 5:20

In this verse, the prophet Isaiah is portraying one of the transgressions committed by the Jewish people, which ultimately contributed to the downfall of the Northern Kingdom by the Assyrians in 720 BC and later led to the demise of the Southern Kingdom by the Babylonians in 586 BC. Moreover, this was not the sole wrongdoing highlighted in this passage; there were additional offenses (such as engaging in immoral festivities,

---

[5]   Mazzalongo, *The Wrong Side of History: Gay Marriage.*

indulging in alcohol, practising corruption and deceit, and displaying arrogance towards God). While these transgressions were grave on their own, in verse 20, Isaiah delineates more than just a single sinful act; he depicts the state of a sinful nation that had deteriorated to the point where they not only embraced and propagated what was essentially wicked but also condemned and mislabelled what had been traditionally considered virtuous.

Isaiah was conveying to the people that they had entirely flipped the moral framework, and consequently, God would administer punishment for their actions. It was not just a matter of failing to adhere to or abide by God's moral principles, a common occurrence throughout history. What set this situation apart was the endeavour to fundamentally alter the very structure itself, whereby sinfulness was now deemed permissible, and virtues such as holiness, faith, and obedience were to be discarded and disdained.

Isaiah cautioned them that treading this path would inevitably lead to their downfall. This demise was on the horizon because once they utterly rejected God's established moral framework and attempted to replace it with their own, they would lose their significance as His chosen people. While striving but falling short of adhering to God's directives still allowed them to rely on His mercy and power for sustenance and deliverance, this approach would be acceptable to God. However, forging their own rules and moral structure, as evidenced by historical precedent, would ultimately result in the downfall of their nation.

Furthermore, Isaiah addressed those individuals who opted to alter the moral framework established by God and upheld by humanity for countless millennia in the following manner:

> Woe to those who are wise in their own eyes And clever in their own sight!
>
> - Isaiah 5:21

This concept can also be extended to the act of codifying within legislation a fresh criterion for determining what is morally acceptable or unacceptable, not only in the context of marriage but also in matters concerning sexual expression.[6]

7.2 Islam, Sexual Ethics, and Homosexuality

The fundamental scriptures of Islam discuss and generally disapprove of sexual relationships between individuals of the same gender. Although the Qur'an does not directly provide specific laws on this issue, it strongly conveys its aversion to the men of the community of Lut who desired same-sex relationships, as evident in its repeated references to their story.

Islam's conservative perspective on matters of sexual immorality, including homosexuality, has posed a significant challenge for these progressive governments. The resolute and steadfast stance of Islam regarding these subjects shines as a guiding light and a final refuge for humanity.

In the Qur'an, chapter 21, verse 107, it states:

وَمَآ أَرْسَلْنَٰكَ إِلَّا رَحْمَةً لِّلْعَٰلَمِينَ

And We have sent you (O Muhammad) not but as a mercy for the 'Alamin (mankind, jinn, and all that exists)

- Al-Anbya: 107

With the growing acceptance of homosexuality through legalization and Islam's unwavering position on this matter, the relevance of this verse becomes more apparent. It's important to recognize that not only is the Prophet Muhammad a blessing to the world, but his message of Islam, with

---

[6]   Mazzalongo, *The Wrong Side of History: Gay Marriage.*

its moral strength and stance on various issues that impact humanity, is equally a source of blessing.

It should be evident that homosexuality is regarded as a sinful and disgraceful behavior. In Islamic terminology, it is referred to as 'Al-Fahsha,' signifying an abhorrent and indecent act. Islam's teachings emphasize that believers should abstain from engaging in such indecent acts and should not contribute to their spread.[7] Allah says:

إِنَّ ٱلَّذِينَ يُحِبُّونَ أَن تَشِيعَ ٱلْفَـٰحِشَةُ فِى ٱلَّذِينَ ءَامَنُوا لَهُمْ عَذَابٌ أَلِيمٌ فِى ٱلدُّنْيَا وَٱلْآخِرَةِ وَٱللَّهُ يَعْلَمُ وَأَنتُمْ لَا تَعْلَمُونَ

Those who love (to see) obscenity published broadcast among the Believers will have a grievous Penalty in this life and the Hereafter: Allah knows, and you know not.

- Al-Nur: 19

7.2.1 Qur'an's Stance on Homosexual Organizations

Sexual disorders and matters concerning gender, specifically referring to the Lesbian, Gay, Bisexual, and Transgender (LGBT) community, are not novel subjects.[8] The Qur'an recounts the tale of the "people of Lut," who faced divine retribution due to their persistent wrongdoing. Simultaneously, both the Quran and the hadith unequivocally condemn homosexual activities, with certain hadith even prescribing capital punishment for those openly involved in male- homosexual or lesbian relations. Consequently,

---

[7]   *Islam's Stance on Homosexual Organizations.* Fiqh, Encouraging the right and Forbidding the wrong. Accessed July 21, 2023. Islamonline. URL: https://fiqh. islamonline.net/en/islams-stance-on-homosexual-organizations/.

[8]   Md Yusof et al., *'Hadith Sahih On Behaviour Of LGBT (Lesbian, Gay, Biseksual And Transgender)'.*

homosexuality is deemed a detestable act, as explicitly mentioned in both the Qur'an and Hadith. A few of the relevant verses are as follows.

In Surah Surah al-Araf, verses 80-84, Allah also says:[9]

وَلُوطًا إِذْ قَالَ لِقَوْمِهِ أَتَأْتُونَ ٱلْفَٰحِشَةَ مَا سَبَقَكُم بِهَا مِنْ أَحَدٍ مِّنَ ٱلْعَٰلَمِينَ

And [We had sent] Lot when he said to his people, Do you commit such immorality as no one has preceded you with from among the worlds?

- Al-A'raf: 80

إِنَّكُمْ لَتَأْتُونَ ٱلرِّجَالَ شَهْوَةً مِّن دُونِ ٱلنِّسَآءِ ۚ بَلْ أَنتُمْ قَوْمٌ مُّسْرِفُونَ

Indeed, you approach men with desire, instead of women. Rather, you are a transgressing people.

- Al-A'raf: 81

وَمَا كَانَ جَوَابَ قَوْمِهِ إِلَّا أَن قَالُوٓا أَخْرِجُوهُم مِّن قَرْيَتِكُمْ ۖ إِنَّهُمْ أُنَاسٌ يَتَطَهَّرُونَ

But the answer of his people was only that they said, "Evict them from your city! Indeed, they are men who keep themselves pure.

- Al-A'raf: 82

فَأَنجَيْنَٰهُ وَأَهْلَهُ إِلَّا ٱمْرَأَتَهُ كَانَتْ مِنَ ٱلْغَٰبِرِينَ

---

[9]   *Islam's Stance on Homosexual Organizations.*

So, We saved him and his family, except for his wife; she was one of those who remained [with the evildoers].

- Al-A'raf: 83

وَأَمْطَرْنَا عَلَيْهِم مَّطَرًا ۖ فَٱنظُرْ كَيْفَ كَانَ عَـٰقِبَةُ ٱلْمُجْرِمِينَ

And We rained upon them a rain [of stones]. Then see how the end of the criminals was.

- Al-A'raf: 84

In Surah Al- Ankaboot:28-35, Allah also says:

وَلُوطًا إِذْ قَالَ لِقَوْمِهِ إِنَّكُمْ لَتَأْتُونَ ٱلْفَـٰحِشَةَ مَا سَبَقَكُم بِهَا مِنْ أَحَدٍ مِّنَ ٱلْعَـٰلَمِينَ

(And (remember) Lut: behold, he said to his people: 'Ye do commit lewdness, such as no people in Creation (ever) committed before you.

- Al- Ankaboot:28

أَئِنَّكُمْ لَتَأْتُونَ ٱلرِّجَالَ وَتَقْطَعُونَ ٱلسَّبِيلَ وَتَأْتُونَ فِى نَادِيكُمُ ٱلْمُنكَرَ ۖ فَمَا كَانَ جَوَابَ قَوْمِهِ
إِلَّا أَن قَالُوا ٱئْتِنَا بِعَذَابِ ٱللَّهِ إِن كُنتَ مِنَ ٱلصَّـٰدِقِينَ

Do ye indeed approach men, and cut off the highway? and practice wickedness (even) in your councils? But his people did not answer but this: they said: 'Bring us the Wrath of Allah if thou tell the truth.'

- Al- Ankaboot:29

قَالَ رَبِّ ٱنصُرْنِى عَلَى ٱلْقَوْمِ ٱلْمُفْسِدِينَ

He said: 'O my Lord! Help Thou me against people who do mischief!'

- Al- Ankaboot:30

وَلَمَّا جَاءَتْ رُسُلُنَآ إِبْرَٰهِيمَ بِٱلْبُشْرَىٰ قَالُوٓا إِنَّا مُهْلِكُوٓا أَهْلِ هَـٰذِهِ ٱلْقَرْيَةِ إِنَّ أَهْلَهَا كَانُوا ظَـٰلِمِينَ

When Our Messengers came to Abraham with the good news, they said: 'We are indeed going to destroy the people of this township: for truly they are (addicted to) crime.'

- Al- Ankaboot:31

قَالَ إِنَّ فِيهَا لُوطًا قَالُوا نَحْنُ أَعْلَمُ بِمَن فِيهَا لَنُنَجِّيَنَّهُ وَأَهْلَهُ إِلَّا ٱمْرَأَتَهُ كَانَتْ مِنَ ٱلْغَـٰبِرِينَ

He said: 'But there is Lut there.' They said: 'Well do we know who is there: We will certainly save him and his following-except his wife: she is one of those who lag behind!'

- Al- Ankaboot:32

وَلَمَّآ أَن جَاءَتْ رُسُلُنَا لُوطًا سِيٓءَ بِهِمْ وَضَاقَ بِهِمْ ذَرْعًا وَقَالُوا لَا تَخَفْ وَلَا تَحْزَنْ إِنَّا مُنَجُّوكَ وَأَهْلَكَ إِلَّا ٱمْرَأَتَكَ كَانَتْ مِنَ ٱلْغَـٰبِرِينَ

And when Our Messengers came to Lut, he was grieved on their account, and felt powerless (to protect) them: but they said: 'Fear thou not, nor grieve we are (here) to save thee and thy following, except thy wife: she is of those who lag.

- Al- Ankaboot:33

إِنَّا مُنزِلُونَ عَلَىٰ أَهْلِ هَـٰذِهِ ٱلْقَرْيَةِ رِجْزًا مِّنَ ٱلسَّمَآءِ بِمَا كَانُوا يَفْسُقُونَ

For we are going to bring down on the people of this township a punishment from heaven because they have been wickedly rebellious.'

- Al- Ankaboot:34

وَلَقَد تَّرَكْنَا مِنْهَآ ءَايَةًۢ بَيِّنَةً لِّقَوْمٍ يَعْقِلُونَ

And We have left thereof an evident Sign, for any people who (care to) understand.

- Al- Ankaboot:35

Furthermore, Surah Ash-Shu'ara - 165 and 166:

أَتَأْتُونَ ٱلذُّكْرَانَ مِنَ ٱلْعَـٰلَمِينَ

Of all the creatures in the world will ye approach males

- Ash-Shu'ara: 165

وَتَذَرُونَ مَا خَلَقَ لَكُمْ رَبُّكُم مِّنْ أَزْوَٰجِكُم ۚ بَلْ أَنتُمْ قَوْمٌ عَادُونَ

And leave those whom Allah has created for you to be your mates? Nay ye are a people transgressing (all limits)!

- Ash-Shu'ara: 166

The end result of not giving up on homosexuality is destruction.

فَلَمَّا جَآءَ أَمْرُنَا جَعَلْنَا عَـٰلِيَهَا سَافِلَهَا وَأَمْطَرْنَا عَلَيْهَا حِجَارَةً مِّن سِجِّيلٍ مَّنضُودٍ

When Our decree was issued, We turned (the cities) upside down and rained down on them brimstones hard as baked clay spread layer on layer

- Surah Hud: 82

مُّسَوَّمَةً عِندَ رَبِّكَ وَمَا هِىَ مِنَ ٱلظَّـٰلِمِينَ بِبَعِيدٍ

Marked as from thy Lord: nor are they ever far from those who do wrong!

- Surah Hud: 83

In these remarkable verses, Allah, the Supreme, illuminated the deeds of the people of Lut, characterizing them as "abominable" [lewd, atrocious], and their settlements were labeled as places that practiced "wickedness." Additionally, it's established that the term "fahisha" (abominable) in this context pertains to the act of adultery, encompassing the deeds committed by the people of Lut, involving (male) sodomy and (female) lesbianism.[10]

Furthermore, significant transgressions akin to those committed by the people of Lut typically result in punishment in the Hereafter, as this retribution surpasses the consequences in the mortal realm, and the disgrace in the Hereafter outweighs that of the present world. Additionally, the penalties in the Hereafter, such as facing the Hellfire and enduring Allah's curse – may Allah protect us from it – and being excluded from

---

[10]   Md Yusof et al., 'Hadith Sahih On Behaviour Of LGBT (Lesbian, Gay, Biseksual And Transgender)'; Islam's Stance on Homosexual Organizations.

Allah's mercy, inflict greater harm and suffering than any conceivable worldly punishment.[11]

The scholars of the Ummah (Muslim community) unanimously concur, drawing from the teachings of the Qur'an and authenticated Prophetic Tradition (Sunnah), in the unequivocal prohibition of both practices – homosexuality and lesbianism. These prohibitions are grounded in the understanding that both behaviours intrinsically challenge a person's inherent humanity, disrupt the family structure, and clash with the intentions of the Divine Lawgiver. One of these intentions is the establishment of natural sexual inclinations between males and females to promote the institution of marriage.[12]

In Islam, the primary purpose of marriage is not centered around fulfilling sexual desires; rather, it serves as a vehicle to attain inner tranquillity and actualize the bond of love and compassion between spouses. Moreover, marriage functions as a means for the continuation of human existence and the cultivation of strong relationships that contribute to the formation of healthy families – the foundational units of society. Islam's ultimate objective revolves around fostering a thriving and virtuous society. Unlike animals driven solely by sexual instincts, human beings possess the capacity to govern their desires and choose how to channel them. This ability, along with the gift of free will, sets them apart from other creatures, enabling them to align their behaviours with goodness and righteousness. Hence, viewing mere sensual gratification as an end contradicts one's innate nature and deviates from the natural order.[13]

Moreover, the prevailing confusion regarding matters related to the Hereafter and other facets contributes to the perplexity surrounding sexuality, thereby giving rise to a state of disorder. This state of disorder has led to the proliferation of avarice and insatiability, prompting the establishment of various industries aimed at inciting passions. This includes the creation of sexual tourism, the production of explicit films, the

---

[11]   *Islam's Stance on Homosexual Organizations.*
[12]   Ibid.
[13]   Ibid.

promotion of devices intended for sensual gratification, and other similar ventures. Consequently, the very notion of family and its fundamental values have been eroded, leading to a blurred understanding of appropriate relationships between individuals of different genders. The outcome has even reached a point where we witness the formation of families comprised of two males or two females.[14]

In their commentaries on Allah's words:

وَاللَّاتِي يَأْتِينَ الْفَاحِشَةَ مِن نِّسَآئِكُمْ فَاسْتَشْهِدُوا عَلَيْهِنَّ أَرْبَعَةً مِّنكُمْ ۖ فَإِن شَهِدُوا فَأَمْسِكُوهُنَّ فِي الْبُيُوتِ حَتَّىٰ يَتَوَفَّاهُنَّ الْمَوْتُ أَوْ يَجْعَلَ اللَّهُ لَهُنَّ سَبِيلًا ٤:١٥ وَالَّذَانِ يَأْتِيَانِهَا مِنكُمْ فَآذُوهُمَا ۖ فَإِن تَابَا وَأَصْلَحَا فَأَعْرِضُوا عَنْهُمَا ۗ إِنَّ اللَّهَ كَانَ تَوَّابًا رَّحِيمًا ٤:١٦

If any of your women are guilty of lewdness, Take the evidence of four (Reliable) witnesses from amongst you against them; and if they testify, confine them to houses until death do claim them, or Allah ordain for them some (other) way. If two men among you are guilty of lewdness, punish them both. If they repent and amend, leave them alone; for Allah is Oft-returning, Most Merciful.

- An-Nisa:15-16

Certain scholars have asserted that the term "Al-lati" in the verse refers to lesbians engaging in deviant behaviour among themselves, while the term "Al-ladhani" signifies homosexuals participating in similar behaviour among themselves. The punishment for their actions involves both verbal condemnation and actual consequences.[15]

7.2.2 Hadith Concerning LGBT

For any challenges that humanity faces, the primary guidance should be sought from the al-Qur'an and al-Hadith. This is because al-Hadith,

---

[14]   Ibid.

[15]   *Islam's Stance on Homosexual Organizations.*

as the secondary source in Islam, has played a significant role in shaping the cultural landscape of Islamic civilization from the time of Prophet Muhammad (PBUH) and his companions to the present day. This influence spans across aspects such as belief, worship, morals, and mu'amalat (interpersonal dealings). Imam Ahmad emphasized that al-hadith is the essential avenue for studying Islamic law and regulations. Relying solely on the Qur'an to comprehend its verses and derive its rulings, without drawing support from al-hadith, can lead one astray and hinder the fulfilment of their life's purpose. Consequently, acts like homosexuality (sodomy and al-sihaq) and the discussion about women who resemble men and men who resemble women (al-mutasyabbih) have also been addressed in al-Hadith.

Numerous hadiths distinctly elucidate the prohibition and admonition against LGBT behaviours. Within the hadith, the concept of same-gender sexual orientation or homosexuality is articulated through the terms liwat (sodomy) and al-sihaq (lesbianism). A narration by Jaabir (may Allah be pleased with him) states: "The Prophet (peace and blessings of Allah be upon him) said: 'There is nothing I fear for my ummah more than the deed of the people of Loot." In Hadith, the Prophet, peace and blessings be upon him, clarifies the gravity of this abomination by saying: "Allah curses the one who does the actions of the people of Lut" repeating it three times; and he said in another Hadith: "If a man comes upon a man then they are both adulterers"

In this context, he equated homosexuality to adultery in terms of the punishments prescribed by Shari'ah, as it constitutes both an abomination and falls within the definition of adultery. Moreover, reports from the Companions (may Allah be pleased with them) have suggested that this transgression warrants a more severe penalty compared to that of adultery, aiming to ensure its strong deterrent effect. Indeed, the punishment stipulated involves the immolation or stoning to death of both parties involved in the homosexual act (the perpetrator and the recipient), as a reflection of the divine punishment inflicted upon the people of Lut after the obliteration of their community.[16] Ibn Abbas also conveyed a narration wherein the Messenger of Allah proclaimed: "If you find someone engaging in the conduct of the people of Lut, then kill the one who does it and the one to whom it is done." (Hasan)

Regarding lesbians, the Prophet, peace, and blessings be upon him, made a statement concerning them: "If a woman comes upon a woman, they are both Adulteresses." Scholars have discussed that it becomes the responsibility of the governing authority to establish an appropriate reprimand for lesbians in accordance with the seriousness of the offense committed. While some scholars have held differing opinions on these penalties, it is not due to any uncertainty about the fact that such actions constitute a transgression, but rather because of the absence of explicit divine textual prescriptions for worldly sanctions. Nevertheless, the actions of the Prophet's Companions do indicate that this wrongdoing merits a worldly punishment, which is to be implemented by those in a position of authority within the Muslim community. The well-known incident involving Abu Bakr Al-Siddiq and Khalid Ibn Al-Waleed's letter on this matter is widely documented and can be found in various sources.[17]

The account alluded to is recounted as follows: "In his work 'Fat-h al-Qadir,' the renowned Hanafi scholar Ibn al-Humam states: Al-Bayhaqi reported in his book 'Shu'ab al-Iman' based on Abu ad-Dunya's narration of Abd al-'Aziz ibn Abi Hazim, who related from Dawud ibn Bakr, who in turn related from Muhammad ibn al-Mukadir the following incident: Khalid Ibn al-Walid wrote to Abu Bakr, seeking a legal ruling regarding a situation where one man had engaged in sexual intercourse with another man. In response, Abu Bakr assembled the Companions of the Prophet, peace and blessings be upon him and sought their opinions. 'Ali, may Allah be pleased with him, took the most stringent stance, declaring, 'Only one nation defied Allah by committing such a sin, and you are aware of how Allah dealt with them. I believe we should burn the man with fire.'

---

[16]   Ibid.
[17]   Ibid.

The Companions were unanimous in their agreement." This event is also documented by al-Waqidi in the section addressing apostasy, found at the conclusion of the portion discussing the apostasy of Bani Salim.[18]

In summary, engaging in such behaviour, whether involving two males or two females, is regarded as an abhorrent act and a transgression. Hence, the assertions made by these immoral individuals are categorically rejected by Islam and hold no validity. Additionally, the fact that certain religious groups may have yielded to pressure and permitted their adherents to partake in such activities cannot be construed as a valid justification for actions that are explicitly prohibited. Throughout history, there have been instances of people altering their faiths by modifying or discarding essential principles. In contrast, Islam maintains a resolute stance on this issue, refusing any form of compromise or concession under any circumstances.[19]

Muslims must exercise caution and guard against the influence of these individuals who deviate from the right path, ensuring that they are not granted any chance to mingle with and corrupt their children. It is crucial to recognize that they are unfit to establish mosques or participate in their activities, and they are equally unsuitable to lead those who attend these places of worship, regardless of their affiliations. Instead of ridiculing and belittling the beliefs and emotions of Muslims, their priority should be to seek remedies for their own distortions, cleanse their souls from any impurities, and redirect themselves onto a virtuous course.[20]

7.2.3 Modern Islamic Scholars View

As the prohibition originates from his God, a Muslim should not delay medical evidence to establish harm in engaging in what Allah has forbidden. Instead, they should firmly believe that Allah only commands what is

---

[18]   Ibid.
[19]   Ibid.
[20]   *Islam's Stance on Homosexual Organizations.*

beneficial for humanity, and these contemporary revelations should only strengthen their conviction and trust in the profound wisdom of Allah.[21]

Ibn Al Qayyim

Ibn al-Qayyim said: "Both of them – fornication and homosexuality – involve immorality that goes against the wisdom of Allah's creation and commandment. For homosexuality involves innumerable evil and harms, and the one to whom it is done would be better off being killed than having this done to him, because after that he will become so evil and so corrupt that there can be no hope of his being reformed, and all good is lost for him, and he will no longer feel any shame before Allah or before His creation. The semen of the one who did that to him will act as a poison on his body and soul. The scholars differed as to whether the one to whom it is done will ever enter Paradise. There are two opinions which I heard Shaykh al-Islam (may Allah have mercy on him) narrate." (Al-Jawab al-Kafi, p. 115).[22]

Sheikh Muhammed Salih Al-Munajjid

In his contribution, Sheikh Muhammed Salih Al-Munajjid said the act of homosexuality stands as a grave offense, one of the most severe sins, and an act that is deeply repugnant. Allah punished those who engaged in it in a manner distinct from how other communities were punished. It signifies a departure from the natural disposition (fitrah), a clear path of misguidance, a lack of sound reasoning, and a deficiency in religious devotion. Moreover, it serves as an omen of eventual downfall and exclusion from Allah's mercy. We beseech Allah for our protection and well-being.[23]

---

[21] S. M. S. Al-Munajjid. *Why Does Islam Forbid Lesbianism and Homosexuality?* Adultery/fornication and Homosexuality Publication. Accessed July 9, 2023. Islam Q&A, 2009. URL: https://islamqa.info/en/answers/10050/why-does-islam-forbid-lesbianism-and-homosexuality.

[22] *Islam's Stance on Homosexual Organizations*; Al-Munajjid, *Why Does Islam Forbid Lesbianism and Homosexuality?*

[23] M. Al-Munajjid. *The Punishment For Homosexuality.* Adultery/fornication and Homosexuality Publication. Accessed July 9, 2023. Islam Q&A, 2006. URL: https://islamqa.info/en/answers/10050/why-does-islam-forbid-lesbianism-and-homosexuality.

Ibn Al Qayyim

Imaam Ibn al-Qayyim (may Allaah have mercy on him) said: It has been narrated that the Prophet (peace and blessings of Allaah be upon him) stated: "Kill the one who does it and the one to whom it is done." (Reported by the compilers of the Four Sunan collections. Its chain of narration is authentic. At-Tirmidhi remarked that it is a sound hadeeth.).[24]

Abu Bakr al-Siddiq passed judgment in accordance with this, and after consulting with the companions (Sahaabah), he issued instructions to this effect to Khalid. Among the companions, Ali held the strictest stance regarding this matter. Ibn al-Qasaar and our scholar, as well as our mentor, stated that the companions (Sahaabah) unanimously agreed that those who engage in homosexual acts should be put to death, but there were differences in their opinions on the method of execution. Abu Bakr al-Siddiq suggested throwing the offender down from a cliff, while Ali proposed collapsing a wall on them. Ibn Abbas suggested stoning them. This indicates a consensus among the companions that the punishment for such acts should be death, though they disagreed on the specific method of execution. This is reminiscent of the Prophet's ruling (peace and blessings be upon him) concerning individuals who engage in incestuous intercourse. In both cases, sexual relations are strictly prohibited. The linkage between these cases is apparent in the narration of Ibn Abbas (may Allah be pleased with him), who reported the words of the Prophet (peace and blessings be upon him), " Whoever you find doing the deed of the people of Loot, kill them." Similarly, it was reported that the Prophet (peace and blessings be upon him) said, " Whoever has intercourse with a woman who is his mahram, kill him." Another narration with the same chain of narration states, "Whoever

---

[24] M. Salih. *Can those who have committed homosexual acts be forgiven, and is it permissible for such a person to get married?* Adultery/fornication and Homosexuality Publication. Accessed July 9, 2023. Islam Q&A, 2000. URL: https://islamqa.info/en/ answers/.

has intercourse with an animal, kill him and kill the animal with him."
(Narrated by Ahmad, 2420; Abu Dawood, 4464; al-Tirmidhi, 1454; al-
Haakim, 4/355).[25]

To conclude, there is no doubt that Islam's stance on homosexuality
is unequivocal.

---

[25] Ibid.

8. Law and the Balance of Rights Between Homosexuals and Heterosexuals

E ach nation possesses laws that define the rights and responsibilities of both its citizens and the government. Nonetheless, there exists a distinct set of regulations with international recognition known as "Human Rights Law." This universal legal framework is a requirement for every civilized and democratic nation to incorporate into its legislation. The endorsement of homosexuality as a legal matter establishes that individuals identifying as homosexuals are also entitled to these rights.

The underlying principle of Human Rights Law is rooted in the notion that, as humans, we inherently deserve a certain level of dignity and the ability to experience our humanity to its fullest extent. Consequently, we are granted certain rights that are intrinsic and should not be abrogated, except in extraordinary circumstances. This principle is not contingent upon one's identity or characteristics; rather, it asserts that every human is entitled to reap the benefits of this legal framework.

A fundamental aspect of the principle of equality is the prohibition of discrimination. This component ensures that no individual is deprived of their rights based on factors such as race, gender, language, religion, political beliefs, nationality, social background, wealth, or birth circumstances. The right to be free from discrimination is a cornerstone on which individuals with diverse sexual orientations rely to seek acceptance and embrace their identities within society. For instance, the United Kingdom's Equality Act of 2010 incorporates provisions against discrimination, treating all individuals as equals, regardless of their birth circumstances or sexual orientation.

To be equitable, the legislation aimed at preventing discrimination is not inherently problematic. However, concerns arise when governmental bodies exploit this legislation to impose the values of the homosexual community onto individuals whose beliefs and religious practices stand in opposition. While it is justifiable for homosexuals to openly express their sexual orientation without fear or shame, it should also be acknowledged that heterosexual individuals have the right to voice their opinions and live their lives according to their own beliefs and preferences.

The complication frequently arises from the tension between the liberties that this legislation bestows. For instance, the conflict often emerges between the right to non-discrimination and the equally significant principle of freedom of speech, which is a fundamental aspect of human rights. These two rights do not always coexist harmoniously.

Is there any legal safeguard for heterosexual individuals in a society that leans towards supporting the rights of homosexuals? From my perspective, the necessary protection for heterosexuals is inherently encompassed within the framework of the same fundamental human rights principles. Within the United Kingdom, the safeguarding of citizens' human rights is enshrined in the Human Rights Act of 1998. Article 9 of this Act stipulates:

"Everyone has the right to freedom of thought, conscience, and religion; this right includes freedom to change his religion or belief and freedom, either alone or in community with others and in public or private, to manifest his religion or belief, in worship, teaching practice and observance".

The entitlement to freedom of thought, conscience, and religion obligates each person to adhere to the principles and beliefs of their faith. This liberty to live in accordance with one's religious principles is not confined solely to adults but also encompasses minors and individuals of all ages. This is underscored by the United Kingdom Children Act of 2005, as delineated in section 3(1), which stipulates:[1]

"All the rights, duties, powers, responsibilities and authority which by law a parent of a child has concerning the child and his property".

Parents have the following responsibilities for their children.[2]

- The power to determine the child's education and where the child goes to school.
- The power to choose, register, or change the child's name.
- The power to appoint a child's guardian in the event of the death of a parent.
- The power to consent to a child's operation or certain medical treatment.
- The power to access a child's medical records.
- The power to consent to take the child abroad for holidays or extended stays.
- The power to represent the child in legal proceedings.
- The power to determine the religion the child should be brought up with. Where there is a mixed cultural background, this should include exposure to the religions of all those with Parental Responsibility, until the child can reach an age where he/she can make their own decision on this.

[1]   *Parental responsibility*. Family. Accessed July 9, 2023. Child Law Advice, 2006. URL: https://childlawadvice.org.uk/information-pages/parental-responsibility/.
[2]   Ibid.

9. Conclusion

I n conclusion, the scope of Islamic law is broader than the common law or civil law. Hence, for many Muslims, Islam is a complete way of life and the literal meaning is peace, which is usually achieved through submission. This submission is to the laws and regulations as slated by the Qur'an and Sunnah. The Qur'an is the holy scripture of the Muslims which is believed to have been revealed directly to the Prophet Muhammad (PBUH) by Angel Jubril (Gabriel). Despite the fact that the Qur'an was revealed over 1400 years ago, it still applies to modern/ contemporary times. The Qur'an deals with how a Muslim should live his or her life which is what Islamic Law is all about. In addition to core legal doctrines covering the family, wrongs, procedure, and commercial transactions Islamic law also includes detailed rules regulating religious ritual and social etiquette. This book has dealt with Islamic Law and the place it has in the modern/ contemporary legal systems.

Furthermore, as previously mentioned, numerous scientific studies have indicated that genetics play a minor or negligible role in influencing same-sex attraction. The prevailing consensus maintains that the emergence of same-sex attraction is a result of a person's exposure to diverse circumstances and encounters during their upbringing. These factors include growing up in households with absent fathers or where the mother's influence is dominant, and the father's role is weak. Additionally, experiences such as sexual and physical abuse, early exposure to gay pornography, experimentation with same-sex activities during adolescence, feelings of anxiety or sexual confusion, and living in a permissive society that promotes such a lifestyle contribute to the development of same-sex attraction. It is important to note that not everyone exposed to these factors will necessarily experience same-sex attraction, but many of these elements are prevalent among those who do.

Observing that the scientific argument was yielding little progress, the gay movement shifted its strategy to seeking legitimacy through human and civil rights narratives. Portraying themselves as victims of discrimination, they aligned with the human and civil rights movements and applied pressure on governments using this new approach. Therefore, the legalization of homosexuality in the United States, United Kingdom, and Europe cannot be justified based on health anomalies or biological factors. The causal factors behind homosexuality are not rooted in nature but are greatly influenced by nurturing experiences. Numerous experienced psychologists have established that environmental influences play a pivotal role in shaping a child's sexual orientation. If this holds true, then there should exist a potential for a cure for homosexuality. Before various countries legalized and decriminalized homosexuality, there were reported instances of homosexual individuals being reportedly cured through psychological interventions.

Dr. Joseph Nicolosi has outlined a list of potential causes, including a lack of parental affection from same-sex parents, that contribute to homosexual behaviour. These causes stand out as plausible explanations for such behaviour. To prevent homosexuality in children, a significant responsibility rests with parents to ensure comprehensive emotional guidance. This involves ensuring the presence of both male and female parental figures in a child's life. It's widely recognized that divorce has a profound impact on children, often more so than on the parents themselves. One consequence that can arise from divorce is homosexuality.

Regarding the legal aspect, I have concerns that addressing the issue might be challenging due to the legal framework that safeguards both heterosexuals and homosexuals. My reservations about relying on the legal system stem from the hierarchy of laws within our judicial system. Human rights law is considered the paramount law, taking precedence over all other regulations. Consequently, whenever a conflict arises between human rights law and other legislations, human rights law supersedes the latter. This raises questions about how conflicts between different sections of human rights law would be resolved. The current scenario illustrates a conflict between the rights of homosexuals and heterosexuals, without a clear resolution in sight. As a result, one group's rights can inadvertently oppress the other group.

Furthermore, it is anticipated that this book will serve as a comprehensive resource for advocates of the LGBT movement, enlightening them about the unequivocal rejection of their unconventional conduct within the framework of Islam. Homosexuality is a sinful act in Islam, as opposed to a form of identity which is now a dominant perspective propagated in western societies. Equally important, the apprehension of divine punishment, exemplified by the fate of the people of Lut, should be taken as a grave reminder and a point for introspection, encouraging a complete avoidance of LGBT behaviour. Individuals should distance themselves from such actions, recognizing that if a person engaged in this wrongdoing (homosexuality), or any other act subject to hadd punishment, genuinely repents to Allah, ceases the sinful behaviour, seeks forgiveness, feels remorse for their actions, and resolves never to revert, their repentance will be accepted by Allah.

In Surah Al-Furqan: 68-71, Allaah says:

وَٱلَّذِينَ لَا يَدْعُونَ مَعَ ٱللَّهِ إِلَٰهًا ءَاخَرَ وَلَا يَقْتُلُونَ ٱلنَّفْسَ ٱلَّتِى حَرَّمَ ٱللَّهُ إِلَّا بِٱلْحَقِّ وَلَا يَزْنُونَ وَمَن يَفْعَلْ ذَٰلِكَ يَلْقَ أَثَامًا

And those who invoke not any other ilaah (god) along with Allaah, nor kill such person as Allaah has forbidden, except for just cause, nor commit illegal sexual intercourse and whoever does this shall receive the punishment.

- Al-Furqan:68

يُضَـٰعَفْ لَهُ ٱلْعَذَابُ يَوْمَ ٱلْقِيَـٰمَةِ وَيَخْلُدْ فِيهِ مُهَانًا

The torment will be doubled to him on the Day of Resurrection, and he will abide therein in disgrace;

- Al-Furqan:69

إِلَّا مَن تَابَ وَءَامَنَ وَعَمِلَ عَمَلًا صَـٰلِحًا فَأُولَـٰئِكَ يُبَدِّلُ ٱللَّهُ سَيِّـَٔاتِهِمْ حَسَنَـٰتٍ وَكَانَ ٱللَّهُ غَفُورًا رَّحِيمًا

Except those who repent and believe (in Islamic Monotheism), and do righteous deeds; for those, Allaah will change their sins into good deeds, and Allaah is Oft-Forgiving, Most Merciful.

- Al-Furqan:70

وَمَن تَابَ وَعَمِلَ صَـٰلِحًا فَإِنَّهُ يَتُوبُ إِلَى ٱللَّهِ مَتَابًا

And whosoever repents and does righteous good deeds; then verily, he repents towards Allaah with true repentance

- Al-Furqan:71

In addition, Surah Az-Zumar: 53 says:

> قُلْ يَـٰعِبَادِىَ ٱلَّذِينَ أَسْرَفُوا عَلَىٰ أَنفُسِهِمْ لَا تَقْنَطُوا مِن رَّحْمَةِ ٱللَّهِ ۚ إِنَّ ٱللَّهَ يَغْفِرُ ٱلذُّنُوبَ جَمِيعًا ۚ إِنَّهُۥ هُوَ ٱلْغَفُورُ ٱلرَّحِيمُ

> O My servants who have transgressed against themselves [by sinning], do not despair of the mercy of Allah. Indeed, Allah forgives all sins. Indeed, it is He who is the Forgiving, the Merciful."
>
> - Az-Zumar: 53

To conclude, Muslims living in the diaspora should safeguard their faith diligently and make it a priority to instill the teachings of Islam in their children. This is crucial, as Islamic teachings are the guiding light that can counteract the negative influences of homosexuality.

Bibliography

2022 Report on International Religious Freedom: Malaysia. Report. Accessed July 9, 2024. U.S. Department of State, 2022. URL: https://www.state.gov/reports/2022-report-on-international-religious-freedom/malaysia/#:~:text=A%20non-Muslim%20wishing%20to,faith%20without%20explicit%20parental%20permission..

Ahmed. scholars.

Ajijola, A. *Introduction to Islamic Law*. Adam Publishers & Distributors, 2007. ISBN: 9788174354266.

Al-Bukhari. Hadith 2109.

Al-Arba 'ina Hadithan An-Nawawiyyah. Hadith 14.

Al-Arba 'ina Hadithan An-Nawawiyyah. Hadith 24.

Al-Bukhari and Muslim (www.eaalim.com>Home>Blog). Hadith.

Al-Misri, A. I.-N. *The Reliance of the Traveller (edited and translated by Nuh Ha Mim Keller)*. Amana Publications, 1994.

Al-Munajjid, M. *The Punishment For Homosexuality*. Adultery/fornication and Homosexuality Publication. Accessed July 9, 2023. Islam Q&A, 2006. URL: https://islamqa.info/en/answers/10050/why-does-islam-forbid-lesbianism-and-homosexuality.

Al-Munajjid, S. M. S. *Why Does Islam Forbid Lesbianism and Homosexuality?* Adultery/fornication and Homosexuality Publication. Accessed July 9,

2023. Islam Q&A, 2009. URL: https://islamqa.info/en/answers/10050/ why-does-islam-forbid-lesbianism-and-homosexuality.

Allen, L. S. and R. A. Gorski. "Sexual orientation and the size of the anterior commissure in the human brai." In: *Proceedings of the National Academy of Sciences of the United States of America* 89 15 (1992), pp. 7199–202. DOI: https://doi.org/10.1073/pnas.89.15.7199. URL: https:// pubmed.ncbi.nlm.nih.gov/1496013/.

Badr, G. M. "Islamic Law: Its Relation to Other Legal Systems". In: *The American Journal of Comparative Law* 26.2 (Apr. 1978), pp. 187–198. ISSN: 0002-919X. DOI: 10.2307/839667. eprint: https:// academic.oup. com/ajcl/article-pdf/26/2/187/10481802/ajcl0187.pdf. URL: https://doi. org/10.2307/839667.

Balthazart, J. "Minireview: Hormones and human sexual orientation." In: *Endocrinology* 152 8 (2011), pp. 2937–2947. URL: https://www.ncbi.nlm. nih.gov/pmc/articles/ PMC3138231/.

Baughey-Gill, S. "When Gay Was Not Okay with the APA: A Historical Overview of Homosexuality and its Status as Mental Disorder". In: 2011. URL: https://cedar.wwu.edu/ orwwu/vol1/iss1/2.

Breedlove, S. M. "Prenatal Influences on Human Sexual Orientation: Expectations versus Data". In: *Seattle J. Soc. Just.* 46.6 (Feb. 2017), 1583– 1592. DOI: 10.1007/s10508-016-0904-2. URL: https://digitalcommons. law.seattleu.edu/sjsj/vol2/iss2/24/.

Bulugh al Maram. Hadith 1285.

Byne, W. "Interview: The Biological Evidence for Homosexuality Reappraised". In: *Issues in Religion and Psychotherapy* 19.1 (1993), pp. 17–27. URL: https://scholarsarchive.byu.edu/irp/vol19/iss1/3.

Chamberlain, G. "A Religious Argument for Same-Sex Marriage". In: *Seattle J. Soc. Just.* 2.2 (Mar. 2004), pp. 494–503. URL: https://digitalcommons. law.seattleu.edu/sjsj/vol2/iss2/24/.

Chappell, B. *Supreme Court Declares Same-Sex Marriage Legal In All 50 States.* America, News. Accessed July 5, 2023. NPR, 2015. URL:

https://www.npr.org/sections/thetwo-way/2015/06/26/417717613/ supreme-court-rules-all-states-must-allow-same-sex-marriages.

Crotty, J. "Structural causes of the global financial crisis: a critical assessment of the 'new financial architecture'". In: *Cambridge Journal of Economics* 33.4 (July 2009), pp. 563–580. ISSN: 0309-166X. DOI: 10.1093/cje/bep023. eprint: https://academic.oup.com/cje/article-pdf/33/4/563/4818627/bep023.pdf. URL: https://doi.org/10.1093/cje/bep023.

Cundale, S. A. "'HOMOSEXUALITY'. A NEW CHRISTIAN ETHIC By Elizabeth R. Moberly. Published by James Clarke". In: *International Journal of Social Psychiatry* 29.3 (1983), pp. 238–238. DOI: 10.1177/002076408302900317. eprint: https://doi.org/10.1177/002076408302900317. URL: https://doi.org/10.1177/002076408302900317.

Deuraseh, N. "Lawful and unlawful foods in Islamic law focus on Islamic medical and ethical aspects". In: 2009. URL: https://api.semanticscholar.org/CorpusID:37911332.

Drescher, J. and J. Merlino. *American Psychiatry and Homosexuality: An Oral History*. Taylor & Francis, 2012. ISBN: 9781136859939.

Drescher, J. "Queer Diagnoses Parallels and Contrasts in the History of Homosexuality, Gender Variance, and the Diagnostic and Statistical Manual (DSM) Review and Recommendations Prepared for the DSM-V Sexual and Gender Identity Disorders Work Group". In: *FOCUS* 18.3 (2020), pp. 308–335. DOI: 10.1176/appi.focus.18302. eprint: https://doi.org/10.1176/appi.focus.18302. URL: https://doi.org/10.1176/appi.focus.18302.

Ebeniro, C. D. "The Problems of Administration of Justice on Female Offenders in Nigeria". In: *African Journal of Criminology and Justice Studies* 4 (2011), p. 28.

Fagan, P. *Gay Gene or Broken Family?* Tech. rep. Accessed July 15, 2023. The Catholic Thing, 2010. URL: https ://www.thecatholicthing.org/2010/05/27/gay-gene-or-broken-family/.

Fathi, S. *Gods and Religions*. Writers Republic LLC, 2023. ISBN: 9798891004665. URL: https://books.google.pt/books?id=-B3-EAAAQBAJ.

Frank, M. J. ""Trying Times: The Prosecution of Terrorists in the Central Criminal Court of Iraq". In: *Florida Journal of International Law* 18.1 (2006), 71–90. DOI: 10.1257/0895330042162421. URL: https://scholarship.law.ufl.edu/fjil/vol18/iss1/1.

Glenn, H. *Legal Traditions of the World: Sustainable Diversity in Law*. Oxford University Press, 2014. ISBN: 9780199669837.

Haroon, M. *An Integrated Introductory Note on Shari'ah Law*. Tech. rep. 14. Lagos, 2001. Hodgson, M. *The Classical Age of Islam*. The Venture of Islam: Conscience and History in a World Civilization. University of Chicago Press, 2009. ISBN: 9780226346861.

Horrie, C. and P. Chippindale. *What is Islam?: A Comprehensive Introduction*. Virgin, 2007. ISBN: 9780753511947.

Identical Twins Studies Prove Homosexuality is Not Genetic. Featured. Accessed July 13, 2023. The Aquila Report, 2013. URL: https://theaquilareport.com/identical-twins-studies-prove-homosexuality-is-not-genetic/.

II, T. H. M. and N. Zamichow. *Study Ties Part of Brain to Men's Sexual Orientation : Medicine: San Diego researcher's findings offer first evidence of a biological cause for homosexuality*. Science & Medicine. Los Angeles Times, 1991.

Imam Muhammad ibn Idris al-Shafi'I. *Al-Shafiis Risala: Treatise on the Foundations of Islamic Jurisprudence*. The Islamic Text Society, 2010.

Islamic dietary laws. Article. Accessed July 9, 2024. Wikipedia, 2022. URL: https://en.wikipedia.org/wiki/Islamic_dietary_laws#:~:text=Forbidden%20food%20substances%20include%20alcohol,in%20the%20name%20of%20God..

Islam's Stance on Homosexual Organizations. Fiqh, Encouraging the right and Forbidding the wrong. Accessed July 21, 2023. Islamonline. URL: https://fiqh.islamonline.net/en/islams-stance-on-homosexual-organizations/.

james, w. h. "Biological and psychosocial determinants of male and female human sexual orientation". In: *Journal of Biosocial Science* 37.5 (2005), 555–567. DOI: 10.1017/S0021932004007059.

Kamali. "Punishment in Islamic Law: a Critique of The Hudud Bill of Kelantan, Malaysia". In: *Arab Law Quarterly* 13 (1998), pp. 203–234. URL: https://api.semanticscholar.org/CorpusID:53065591.

Kamali, M. *Punishment in Islamic Law: An Enquiry Into the Hudud Bill of Kelantan*. Ilmiah Publisher, 2000. ISBN: 9789832092285.

Khalilieh, H. *Admiralty and Maritime Laws in the Mediterranean Sea (ca. 800-1050): The Kitaˉb Akriyat al-Sufun vis-à-vis the Nomos Rhodion Nautikos*. eng. Vol. 64. Leiden and Boston: Brill, 2006. ISBN: 9789004152533.

Khalilieh, H. *Islamic Maritime Law: An Introduction*. Studies in Islamic law and society. Brill, 1998. ISBN: 9789004109551.

Khan, A. "The Reopening of the Islamic Code: The Second Era of Ijtihad". eng. In: (2003).

Kuran, T. "The Absence of the Corporation in Islamic Law: Origins and Persistence". In: *University of Southern California Center for Law & Social Science (CLASS) Research Paper Series* (2005). URL: https://api. semanticscholar.org/CorpusID:2890366.

— "The logic of financial westernization in the Middle East". In: *Journal of Economic Behavior & Organization* 56.4 (2005). Festschrift in honor of Richard H. Day, pp. 593–615. ISSN: 0167-2681. DOI: https://doi. org/10.1016/j.jebo.2004.04.002. URL: https://www.sciencedirect.com/ science/article/pii/S0167268104001702.

— "Why the Middle East is Economically Underdeveloped: Historical Mechanisms of Institutional Stagnation". In: *Journal of Economic Perspectives* 18.3 (2004), 71–90. DOI: 10.1257/0895330042162421. URL: https://www.aeaweb.org/articles?id=10.1257/0895330042162421.

Lasco, M. S. et al. "A lack of dimorphism of sex or sexual orientation in the human anterior commissure". In: *Brain Research* 936.1 (2002), pp. 95–98. ISSN: 0006-8993. DOI: https://doi.org/10.1016/

S0006-8993(02)02590-8. URL: https://www.sciencedirect.com/science/article/pii/S0006899302025908.

Legal Literature And Institutions, Jurisprudence: The "sources" Of The Law, The Modern Period. Islamic Law. Accessed July 9, 2023. JRank. URL: https://science.jrank.org/pages/7816/Law-Islamic.html#ixzz8fnRYTPrU.

LeVay, S. "A Difference in Hypothalamic Structure Between Heterosexual and Homosexual Men". In: *Science* 253.5023 (1991), pp. 1034–1037. DOI: 10.1126/science.1887219. eprint: https ://www.science.org/doi/pdf/10.1126/science.1887219. URL: https://www.science.org/doi/abs/10.1126/science.1887219.

Lewes, K. *The Psychoanalytic Theory of Male Homosexuality*. Wilensky-Ritzenhein Gay Book Collection. Simon and Schuster, 1988. ISBN: 9780671623913.

Lippman, M., S. McConville, and M. Yerushalmi. *Islamic Criminal Law and Procedure: An Introduction*. Bloomsbury Academic, 1988. ISBN: 9780275930097.

Mahadi, A., J. E. Saba' Radwan, and L. Burhanuddin. "Shariah View on Consumption Tax: Malaysian GST and SST as Case Studies." In: *Malaysian Journal of Consumer and Family Economics* 22 (2019), pp. 1–14. URL: https://majcafe.com/wp-content/uploads/2022/11/Article-3-Vol-22-2019.pdf.

Makdisi, G. "Scholasticism and Humanism in Classical Islam and the Christian West". In: *Journal of the American Oriental Society* 109.2 (1989), pp. 175–182. ISSN: 00030279. URL: http://www.jstor.org/stable/604423 (visited on 07/13/2024).

Makdisi 1999.

Marriage Equality: Global Comparisons. Backgrounder, News. Accessed July 8, 2023. The Council on Foreign Relations (CFR), 2022. URL: https://www.cfr.org/backgrounder/marriage-equality-global-comparisons.

Mazzalongo, M. *The Wrong Side of History: Gay Marriage*. Review. Accessed July 9, 2023. BibleTalk.tv, 2015. URL: https://bibletalk.tv/the-wrong-side-of-history.

McLaughlin, M. "Is There a Gay Brain? The Problems with Scientific Research of Sexual Orientation". In: *The Great Lakes Journal of Undergraduate History* 6.1 (2018), pp. 45–59. URL: https://scholar.uwindsor.ca/gljuh/vol6/iss1/4.

Md Yusof, M. I. bin et al. *'Hadith Sahih On Behaviour Of LGBT (Lesbian, Gay, Biseksual And Transgender)'*. Booklet: Accessed July 9, 2023. Department of Islamic Development Malaysia (JAKIM), 2015. URL: https://www.islam.gov.my/images/ePenerbitan/Hadis-hadis_Sahih_Berkaitan_Perlakuan_LGBT_BI.pdf.

Morgan, K. S. and R. M. Nerison. "Homosexuality and psychopolitics: An historical overview." In: *Psychotherapy* 30 (1993), pp. 133–140. DOI: https://doi.org/10.1037/0033-3204.30.1.133. URL: https://psycnet.apa.org/record/1994-25249-001.

Muslim Arbitration Tribunal.

Nawawi 3 related by Al-Bukhari and Muslim on authority of Abdullah, the son of Umar Al-Khattab. Hadith 3.

Nawawi 38 related by Al-Bukhari on the authority of Abu Hurayrah. Hadith 38.

Omar, A. M. *Dictionary of the Holy Qur'an*. NOOR Foundation International Inc., 2006.

Otto, J. M. *Sharia and National Law in Muslim Countries: Tensions and Opportunities for Dutch and EU Foreign Policy*. Amsterdam University Press, 2008.

— *Sharia and National Law in Muslim Countries: Tensions and Opportunities for Dutch and Eu Foreign Policy*. Amsterdam University Press, 2008.

Parental responsibility. Family. Accessed July 9, 2023. Child Law Advice, 2006. URL: https://childlawadvice.org.uk/information-pages/parental-responsibility/.

Ramadan, H. *Understanding Islamic Law: From Classical to Contemporary*. Contemporary issues in Islam. AltaMira Press, 2006. ISBN: 9780759109919.

Religion. Tech. rep. Accessed July 11, 2024. 2016. URL: https://techraifa. blogspot.com/2016/12/chapter-1-religion-concept-of-religion.html.

Researcher Simon LeVay Talks About the Science of Sexuality. News. Accessed July 11, 2023. the Office of Marketing and Communications, Elmhurst University, 2012. URL: https://www.elmhurst.edu/news/ researcher-simon-levay-talks-about-the-science-of-sexuality/.

Rizvi, S. M. *Khums, Islamic Tax*. Zakat and Khums (Charity). Accessed July 11, 2024. Al-Islam.Org, 1992. URL: https://www.al-islam.org/printpdf/ book/export/html/11184.

Robinson, F. *The Cambridge Illustrated History of the Islamic World*. Cambridge Illustrated Histories. Cambridge University Press, 1996. ISBN: 9780521669931.

Sahih Al-Bukhari. Hadith 8:82:815.

Sahih Al-Bukhari. Hadith 8:82:826.

Sahih Al-Bukhari. Hadith 8:82:818.

Sahih Al-Bukhari, Sahih Muslim. Hadith.

Salih, M. *Can those who have committed homosexual acts be forgiven, and is it permissible for such a person to get married?* Adultery/fornication and Homosexuality Publication. Accessed July 9, 2023. Islam Q&A, 2000. URL: https://islamqa.info/en/answers/.

Taylor, L. J. *Gay Marriage*. mirrored in the philosophy section: Accessed July 8, 2023. Jonelin, 1999. URL: https://jonelin.tripod.com/politics/ gay.htm.

The attractions of sharia: Nigeria's sharia courts are harsh, but quicker and cleaner than secular ones. Islamic law in Nigeria. Accessed July 9, 2023. The Economist, 2002. URL: https://www.economist.com/ middle-east-and-africa/2002/09/05/the-attractions-of-sharia.

The battle for a religion's heart. Egypt and global Islam. Accessed July 9, 2023. The Economist, 2009. URL: https://www.economist.com/international/2009/08/06/the-battle-for-a-religions-heart.

The Holy Qur'an (103:3).

The Holy Qur'an (16:125).

The Holy Qur'an (16:36).

The Holy Qur'an (17: 26-27).

The Holy Qur'an (17:16).

The Holy Qur'an (17:32).

The Holy Qur'an (17:36).

The Holy Qur'an (18:15).

The Holy Qur'an (21:24).

The Holy Qur'an (2:178).

The Holy Qur'an (21:78-79).

The Holy Qur'an (2:188).

The Holy Qur'an (2:190).

The Holy Qur'an (2:220).

The Holy Qur'an (2:230).

The Holy Qur'an (22:40).

The Holy Qur'an (2:275).

The Holy Qur'an (2:285).

The Holy Qur'an (2:30).

The Holy Qur'an (24:13).

The Holy Qur'an (24:2).

The Holy Qur'an (24:27).

The Holy Qur'an (24:4).

The Holy Qur'an (27:64).

The Holy Qur'an (30:21).

The Holy Qur'an (30:30).

The Holy Qur'an (3:104).

The Holy Qur'an (31:17).

The Holy Qur'an (3:190).

The Holy Qur'an (33:58).

The Holy Qur'an (33:72).

The Holy Qur'an (3:5).

The Holy Qur'an (35:3).

The Holy Qur'an (3:72).

The Holy Qur'an (38:26).

The Holy Qur'an (39:9).

The Holy Qur'an (40:56).

The Holy Qur'an (4:135).

The Holy Qur'an (4:136).

The Holy Qur'an (4:27).

The Holy Qur'an (4:29).

The Holy Qur'an (4:5).

The Holy Qur'an (4:6).

The Holy Qur'an (4:65).

The Holy Qur'an (47:24).

The Holy Qur'an (4:75).

The Holy Qur'an (4:82).

The Holy Qur'an (4:92).

The Holy Qur'an (4:93).

The Holy Qur'an (5:101).

The Holy Qur'an (5:104).

The Holy Qur'an (5:32).

The Holy Qur'an (5:38).

The Holy Qur'an (5:42).

The Holy Qur'an (5:49).

The Holy Qur'an (57:25).

The Holy Qur'an (5:90).

The Holy Qur'an (59:7).

The Holy Qur'an (6:151).

The Holy Qur'an (62:10).

The Holy Qur'an (63:10).

The Holy Qur'an (65:7).

The Holy Qur'an (67:14).

The Holy Qur'an (7:199).

The Holy Qur'an (8:41).

The Holy Qur'an (9:34).

Wardle, L. D. "The Biological Causes and Consequences of Homosexual Behavior and Their Relevance for Family Law and Policies". In: *DePaul Law Review* 56.997 (2006), pp. 997–1034. DOI: https://doi.org/10.1073/pnas.89.15.7199. URL: https://ssrn.com/abstract=2329817.

Weiss, B. *The Spirit of Islamic Law.* Spirit of the laws. University of Georgia Press, 1998. ISBN: 9780820319773.

Wikipedians, B. *Islam.* PediaPress.

Index

www.ingramcontent.com/pod-product-compliance
Lightning Source LLC
Chambersburg PA
CBHW040936030426
42335CB00001B/5